Emilia and the Monument Builder

Emilia and the Monument Builder

REMEMBERING THE SACRIFICE

SM Nostrini

Disclaimer:

This book is a collection of memories and reports. Information gathered has come from a wide variety of sources; newspapers, library archives, academic reports and other digital and online material, and not limited only to the sources acknowledged here. The personal stories and memories by individuals recorded here are their version of events and have been both provided and reproduced in good faith with no disrespect or defamation intended. Every effort has been made to ensure the researched information is correct. No liability for incorrect information or factual errors will be accepted by the author.

A catalogue record for this book is available from the National Library of Australia

ISBN – 9781644403648 (paperback)
ISBN – 9781644402955 (ebook)

Design cover and interior:
Pickawoowoo Publishing Group www.pickawoowoo.com

Printed & channel distribution:
Lightning Source | Ingram (USA/UK/EUROPE/AUS)

Book enquiries:
Email - smnostrini@gmail.com

Images: About the Author - Facebook page SMNostrini

In loving memory of
Jack, Emily, Silvana and Aldo
(Australia)

Franca, Nino and Adriana
(Italia)

Contents

Author's Note

Dear Reader

I had long admired the courage of my mother-in-law, Emily Nostrini, for the challenge she faced to leave her home and family to join her husband on the other side of the world. My respect has grown beyond measure as I discovered details I never knew before.

Our family pride in my father-in-law, Jack Nostrini, for his significant contribution to the construction of the Anzac Desert Mounted Corps Memorial on Mt Clarence continues today. While the heritage listed monument states Harold Hartman as the stonemason, it was in fact, Jack who erected the block work. He was assisted by Adam Rodolewicz and other labourers who worked for Mr Hartman's sub-contract builder, George Hodgson. June Hodgson gave the family several photographs of Jack as he worked on the memorial and some of these are at the back of the book. Harold Hartman, brother of Alice Hartman, owned the stone quarry on Mt Melville. It would seem his business cut and supplied the granite paving slabs that sit between the monument and the surrounding semi-circular wall.

My thanks go to each family member for allowing me to probe their memories to create this story. Special thanks to Rosie and Aldo (sadly, he has since passed away) for all the time they gave me. Aldo's penchant for detail and dates was invaluable. These threads of fact are woven into a fabric of fiction to re-create Jack and Emily's journey written for their descendants. I hope this depiction of their lives will help those who follow to understand their Italian-Australian roots. Other readers may recognise similar stories within their own families and the sacrifices made for a better life other than the one expected in their time.

Where the lines of fact and fiction blur, and where events have not necessarily been used in chronological order, this has been for the sake of storytelling. Some names have been changed, and any fictitious character that resembles a real person is purely coincidental. Regarding historical detail, any errors are mine.

Writing this novel has been a rewarding experience for me. My confidence in pursuing such a task has at times been challenging, but saying that it has also grown me as a person. I have loved the research, reading copious books and accessing the voluminous amount of information available on the internet. I often felt like I was walking alongside Emily and Jack in their experiences, which has been an emotional journey in itself.

I trust I have honoured the two people we have loved dearly and miss daily. I hope you enjoy and appreciate *Emilia and the Monument Builder.*

Acknowledgements

I AM GRATEFUL FOR THE assistance of draft copy proofing by Richard Pittman, Sharron Wise and Audrey Payne. Thanks, Audrey, for our writing mornings in our booth at Dome on Fridays. Also, for the encouragement received from family and close friends, particularly my husband, Steve, to help me persevere with the project to completion.

Albany Summer School writing classes in 2017 and 2018 were positive learning experiences. Input from our Great Southern Writers' Group is valued and appreciated, and I thank my church family for their prayer support.

John 15:12-14 (NIV) "My command is this: Love each other as I have loved you. Greater love has no-one than this, that he lay down his life for his friends. You are my friends if you do what I command."

Love and sacrifice go hand-in-hand. God gave us the greatest example in giving His Son for us. These traits have also been demonstrated in families throughout time, and I thank God for the gift of these actions expressed through the words on these pages.

Emilia in Morbegno

Giovanni in 1942

Main Characters

Del Barba Family:
Lorenzo *(Papa)*
Rosa *(Mama)*
Emilia (Emily)
Giacomo *(Nino)*
Franca
Anna-Maria
Giuliana

Nostrini Family:
Cesare *(Father)* (Chez-uh-ray)
Silvia *(Mother)*
Giovanni (Jack)
Bruno
Francesco
Luigi
Maria
Luciano
Rosanna *(Rosie)*
Cesare *(Cesarino - Ces)*
Silvana *(Sil)*
Steven *(Steve)*
Nadia *(Nard)*

*From **Morbegno:*** (Mor-ben-yo)
Raphael Bartolucci *(Raph)*
Lonconi Brothers
Renato (Alpino)
Guido Della Vedova

*From **Sondrio**:*
Carla Negri
Aldo Scamozzi *(Renzo)*

*From **Genoa:***
Mimi

*From **Somma Lombardo:***
Zio (Uncle) Peppino *(Zio Pino)*
Zia (Aunt) Chiara

*From **Lago di Como:***
Nunzio

*In **Albany:***
Peter and Teresa Caraffa
Geoff and Olive Preston
Bruno and Bruna Rizzi
Alberto D'Alesio *(Albert)*
Patricia Ann Thomas *(Pat)*
Sheryl Lawrence
John Knuiman

MAPS

Part One – Map of Europe

Part Two – Map of Australia

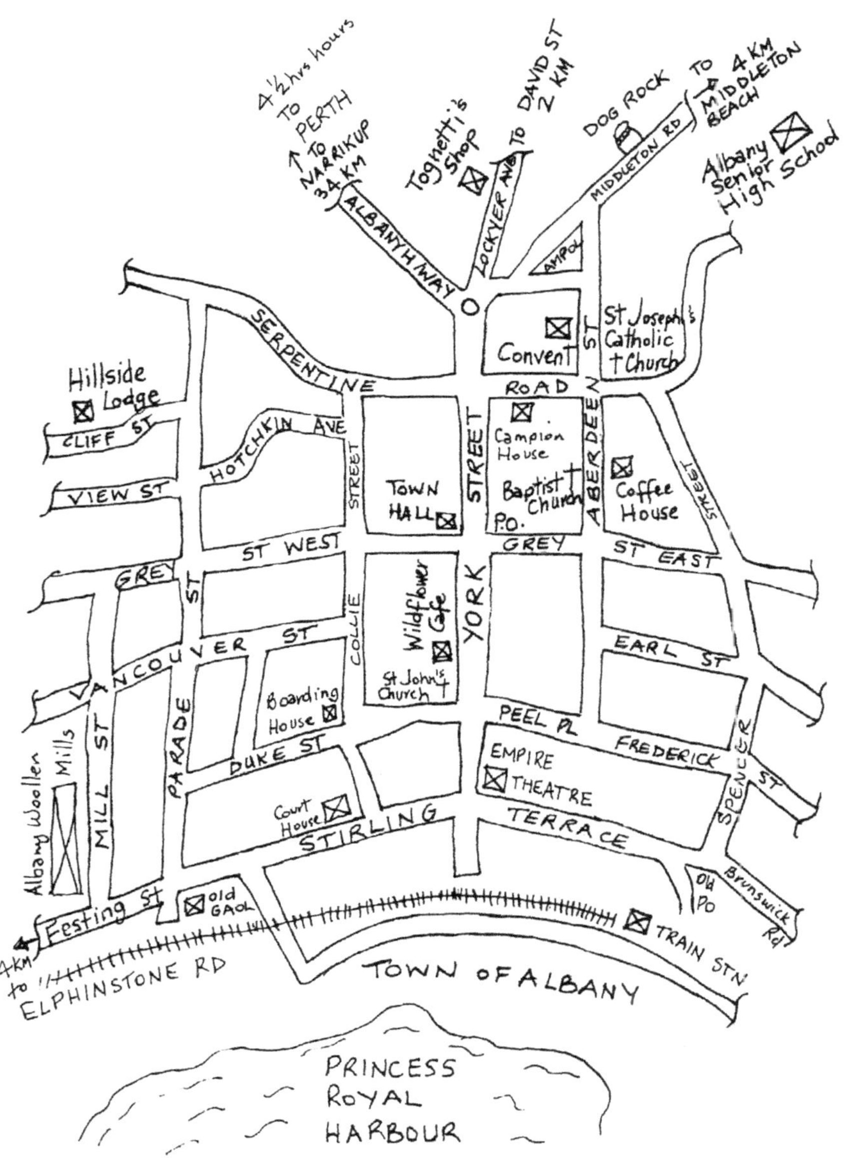

Part Three – Town of Albany

Prologue

Morbegno, Northern Italy

January 13, 1922

The faint odour of paint mingled with wood smoke from the open fire in the next room made Rosa feel nauseous. She glanced out the window through the lace curtain to where snow crystals were illuminated by the moonlight, glistening on the pathway.

Directing her thoughts to her grandparents, who lived upstairs, she remembered they were cousins who had married to keep the property in the family. To her way of thinking it wasn't an ideal reason to unite in matrimony. She was thankful that although her husband wasn't an overly sentimental man, he did love her for herself. Lorenzo's demeanour was much softer after she'd told him she was in the family way.

Another pain wracked through her body, and the attempt to distract her mind with other thoughts was rendered ineffective. Rosa grasped the cotton sheet her mother had tied across the cast iron and enamel bedhead, and hung on tight until the contraction subsided. Her eyes focussed on the framed Madonna on the opposite wall. She prayed for the safe delivery of her baby. Nonna went through childbirth twelve times, and only three of her babies survived. Concerned for the welfare of her child, and frustrated, she groaned as another painful contraction hit.

"Where *is* the midwife?" Rosa said through gritted teeth. "She should be here by now." Her hair was damp with perspiration, and the contractions were one minute apart. The urge to push was almost impossible to control. A few minutes later there was a loud rap at the door announcing the belated appearance of the village midwife. Wiping her thoroughly scrubbed hands on a clean towel, she entered the dimly lit room and smiled at the first time mother.

"Well dear girl, you're almost there. Sorry I'm late. It seems that full moon has caused more than one baby to be born tonight. I've just delivered a boy at the Lonconi house, a brother for little Arnoldo… such lungs, he has a lusty scream and demands to be heard. They called him Marciano." Rosa gave an almighty push, she wasn't interested in some other baby right now.

"Now, let me have a feel. That's good and strong. With the next push the baby's head will be through, and I want you to pant while we ease out the shoulders. All right, you can do this Rosa." A few minutes later a little girl came into the world with a soft cry. Unexpected joyous whoops outside the bedroom door came from the relieved husband, and brand new father, when he realised his first child was born.

"Emilia Assunta Del Barba," Lorenzo proclaimed. He didn't mind that they didn't have a son first, he hoped they would have many more children in the future even though it was quite distressing waiting for the arrival of this one. His teary wife cooed to their pink-cheeked bundle, and put aside all thoughts of the delivery. Rosa was relieved everything was as it should be.

Part One
Italia

CHAPTER ONE

Coming and Going

THE GIRLS BENT DOWN AND took off their shoes to walk up the side path without making any noise. The damp night air clung to their hair, hands and faces; they could barely see each other in the darkness. "Franca, slow down and be quiet, you're crunching the pebbles." Emilia's light step barely moved the smooth round river stones.

"I'm trying to be careful. It sounds loud to you, but no-one else will hear it. I hope Anna-Maria is awake this time. I put a wedge in the window just in case," Franca whispered. It was much easier to open the window from inside their bedroom. Otherwise, they had to push it up while standing on an upturned terracotta pot plant they'd hidden behind the lilac bush. Fortunately, the plant still had enough leaves on it to disguise the pot from being seen by anyone who used the pathway. Franca tapped lightly on the window and waited. Anna-Maria pulled the lace curtain back and opened it.

"You're late! Papa is banking the fire right now."

The girls climbed into the room and gently closed the window. Mama was still knitting, making the click-clack sound as she drew the plain and purl stitches across the length of the metal needles. They jumped into bed and closed their eyes. It was quiet, except for the loud beating of their hearts as they lay fully clothed under the blankets. Mama cracked the door open, as she did every night to peek in and see her daughters sleeping.

"*Buonanotte care ragazze,*" she whispered. Goodnight dear girls.

Emilia felt a shadow of guilt creep across her thoughts for being deceitful; it wasn't like her to be dishonest. After Mama closed the door both she and Franca, slipped out of the big bed they shared to undress and put on their nightgowns. Franca threw her dress, slip, brassiere and woollen stockings over the back of the chair on her side of the bed and put her dressing gown over the top of them. Emilia deftly folded her clothes and stacked them neatly on the box beside the wardrobe. Her old doll sat on top to disguise the pile.

They were as different as chalk and cheese these sisters but loved each other very much in spite of their occasional spats. The girls would come back after chores and breakfast in the morning to put away their best clothes. Franca wouldn't wear her gown in the morning because she was quite happy to wander around in her nightie, even though Papa thought it was most inappropriate.

Emilia lay awake for some time reliving the evening she'd enjoyed, gliding across the smooth wooden floor in Giovanni's embrace. She could still feel the warmth of her small hand in his, and the strength of his upper arms and shoulders as they moved to the beat of the music. She loved to dance, never more than this year.

"Come on sleepy head, stop dreaming about that new boy and get up. We've got to go and milk the cows." Franca shook Emilia awake at the break of day. Cold air came in a rush when they opened the back door to go to the cowshed. The autumn chill deepened as winter approached.

"Just the kind of morning to wear my dressing gown," Franca mumbled under her breath. The cows lowed quietly and chewed on their feed while the girls sat on three-legged stools to milk them.

Thoughts crowded Emilia's mind, last year she'd danced with Raphael Bartolucci. He was tall, a bit gangly and had two left feet for sure. Raph was a nice fellow with dark good looks, and there was a hint from him of wanting to further their relationship, such as it was. Emilia knew he wasn't right for her. She was thankful her parents weren't pressuring her into an arranged marriage, at least not yet. She was sixteen-and-a-half, and to her, that half year was necessary to mention because it made her just that much older.

In the cool cheese preparation room the girls set down the buckets ready to process the milk. While they worked, they chatted. No-one else would interrupt them at this time of day.

"That was too close last night Em," Franca exclaimed. "We could've been caught out, and Papa would be furious. He'd blame me too, even though it's you who wants to go to the dances and meet that new boy."

Turning to look at her sister, Emilia pouted.

"His name is Giovanni, not *new boy*."

She supposed he was a new boy, one of five new boys. It was rare for a whole family to move to their village in the Valtellina. Cesare Nostrini had come to work at the Morbegno Railway Station after the old guard passed away about six months ago. Emilia reminisced about the first time she'd seen Giovanni. He was building a rock wall down at the river bank; there'd been a flood a while ago, not a bad one, but enough for the village mayor to insist on higher retaining walls to hold the banks in case the river flooded again.

Her father was a stone mason, but he was too busy to do the job. She remembered riding her bike towards the *Ponte Ganda* to go to visit a friend who lived on the other side of the river, and that's where it happened. As she approached the bridge, Giovanni had tapped a rock in place, and then looked up. His large, deep-set eyes had locked with hers, and he waved to her with the trowel in his hand and smiled. She had ducked her head down embarrassed he'd noticed her, and an unfamiliar warmth rushed over her at his gesture. Her reverie was interrupted by her sister's prattle.

"Well, I'm surprised we've got away with doing this. It's just as well Nino isn't interested in dancing. You're lucky he'd rather don his hobnail boots, grab a rope and pickaxe and climb up a mountain when he's not holed up in his room studying," Franca went on.

Giacomo was their only brother, but they called him by his preferred name, Nino. If he'd been at the dances, they most certainly would not be. Fortunately, his small room was on the other side of Mama and Papa's. He was the only boy in the family, so he had it to himself. He couldn't hear or see anything from there because if he did he would surely tell Papa – if necessary they would've bribed him to be quiet. No-one in the village would dream of mentioning the dance to their mother in passing at the market because they were aware of how strict Lorenzo was with his daughters.

"I'm sorry I made us late last night. It was hard to leave when I was enjoying myself so much. I recall you seemed to be having quite a time of it yourself," Emilia commented with a tilt of her head and raised eyebrows. Both girls knew their escapades were coming to an end, only two more dances left before winter set in and that would be it for another season.

Giovanni Nostrini was the eldest son in his family, and in the past, he'd often helped his mother when she opened the Tabacchi at the railway station. It was the responsibility of the station guard's wife to manage the small shop when the trains came in during the day. The Tabbachi sold cigarettes, matches, newspapers and postage stamps, among other things.

Ever since Giovanni was ten years old, he'd helped take care of his brothers after school and to make sure they didn't get into mischief while their mother worked in the shop. At other times he ran it for her, especially when his baby sister, Maria, needed to be fed every three hours. They were in Talamona back then, not far from Sondrio. He thought it was good for his mother to have a daughter, not that she had any regrets because she adored her sons. Giovanni's mother was proud of her son, and she knew a particular young lady in the village had stolen his heart. He was waiting for her to be old enough to woo, such was his maturity and sensibility.

The family had been uprooted a few times in the past, originally they'd come from Somma Lombardo. They had been at Gallarate, in the Province of Varese; then Talamona and Morbegno in the Valtellina where it was too far to travel regularly to visit their extended family west of Milano. Morbegno was nestled in the valley between the towering snow-capped Italian mountains. The rushing cloudy blue-green water of melted snow formed the Adda River that flowed past the edge of town. It drained into the northern tip of Lago di Como at Colico. Winter was colder here than in Somma Lombardo, and snow often fell until late in February.

In the summer, lush green farms dotted the valley floor where maize and grain crops swayed in the light breezes. Bright splashes of colour in garden beds, and vivid red and pink geraniums showcased their glory in window boxes at the front of stone houses. Orchards and vegetable patches grew a variety of fresh fruit, grapes, herbs and tomatoes. Some produce was dried or bottled for use throughout the coming winter. Women gathered on winding laneways at a *fontana* to wash clothes where mountain water flowed continuously through concrete troughs. They'd begun to feel at home, and the people had accepted their family into the tight-knit community. Of Giovanni's younger siblings, Luigi was the only brother to have the privilege of a better education. He was in high school and had made friends easily. Maria and Luciano attended the local primary school.

Cesare's position as a station guard was not well paid, but it did provide a flat near the train station at a cheap rate. They were comfortable enough squeezed in together, and were used to the sound of trains during the night. It had always been their lot in life, and when they heard their father leave to attend his platform duties, they would listen for the whistle and then fall straight back to sleep.

Giovanni took any available work to help make ends meet at home. He'd not long finished his time of *naja*, the compulsory attendance of military service for eighteen-year-old males. After World War I, the Government tried to develop more national awareness among its people. Italy had united as a nation in 1861, which was young considering its ancient history. During a good portion of his time in training camp, Giovanni was rostered in the kitchen. He'd been quite content to wield a knife and potato peeler rather than a gun. Many conscripts thought it beneath them to work in the lowly roles of kitchen duty or laundry service because to them it was considered women's work. Some of their provincial dialects were entirely different, so it was a blessing at times that they couldn't understand each other very well. It prevented many hot-headed altercations considering the notorious rivalry of southern and northern Italians. Even though body language and tone demonstrated attitudes, it was difficult to argue when you had no idea of what was said. Throwing arms up in the air and stomping off was a more likely result of the conflict.

When Giovanni's two younger brothers, Bruno and Francesco joined the training unit after their eighteenth birthdays, the commanding officer released Giovanni from his three years' service early. He didn't think it was fair for any mother to have three sons in the military at the same time. Giovanni had missed his family a great deal while he was away, and decided to follow them to the village of Morbegno and make it his home. It was a wise decision in light of his marital prospects.

Planning his future was foremost in his thoughts lately. He needed to find permanent work and save enough money to support a wife. At almost 21, he'd mapped out in his mind what he would do. He had an organised brain and planning was essential to reach his goals. He hoped it would work out, even though it would mean he'd have to go away again for a while.

At Christmas time Giovanni thought he would speak to Emilia to see if she would allow him to approach her father in January, after her seventeenth birthday, to ask his permission to court her. Christmas and New Year was a joyful time, everyone was happy and in good spirits. Surely Emilia's Papa would be agreeable because it would be a year-long courtship. It looked like he would have to go back to Somma Lombardo to get regular employment. They could write to each other and Emilia would be 18 on his return. The separation would be hard but necessary in Giovanni's eyes because he didn't want to risk somebody else taking an interest in his girl. She wasn't his girl yet, but he liked to think of things that way. He knew from the shy looks she gave him when they danced together that Emilia enjoyed his company. He was besotted; she was such a lady, elegant and refined, especially considering how young she was. She'd caught his attention not long after he'd arrived in Morbegno. Several times he'd seen her with her family at church, or with one of her sisters at the market. Giovanni looked forward to the day when he could talk to her, share his thoughts and dreams with her, and be in her company for more time than it took for one dance. He longed for it, patience was a virtue, and virtuous is what he was. The time would come, and it would be worth the wait.

CHAPTER TWO

A Budding Romance

CHRISTMAS APPROACHED, AND SNOWFLAKES FLUTTERED to the ground covering everything in a delicate blanket of white. Candlelight twinkled in festooned shop windows and through the bare branches of trees along the sidewalk. Fresh pine wreaths tied with red ribbons adorned front doors. Decorated rich green fir tree boughs with frosted pine cones sat in the front windows of people's homes. The smell of delicious baking wafted through the streets whenever a door opened. Midnight mass was tomorrow night, time for Giovanni's plan to be put into action.

The church bells tolled their Christmas Eve call to worship and most of the villagers turned out for the *Natale* midnight mass. Giovanni watched for the Del Barba family and managed to slip into the same pew as Emilia. The priest asked the congregation to stand and greet one another in the name of the Lord.

"Peace be with you." They turned to each other and shook hands. Giovanni whispered, "Emilia, can we please talk for a few minutes after the service?"

She nodded as they sat down again. The congregation sang Christmas carols and listened to the story of the virgin birth of Jesus, the Saviour of the world, and the message of love, joy and peace to all mankind.

Throughout the service, Emilia's mind was in a whirl, she tried to listen and sing but struggled to overcome the giddy feeling in response to Giovanni's touch. It had sent a tingling sensation right through her.

She wondered about what he would want to ask her, although she had a fair idea of what might be coming. If he was going to approach the subject of courtship, she knew what her response would be. Emilia had to pull her thoughts together to concentrate on the Eucharist, it was important not to be distracted during that ceremony. The blessing was finally announced, and the mass was over. The young people turned to each other and smiled. Giovanni was utterly mesmerised by the depth in her dark green hazel eyes with golden brown flecks reflecting the light in her soul.

"Emilia, I want your permission to speak to your father and ask him if I can court you. I'll wait until you're 17 in a few weeks' time, and I'll come calling if you agree."

"You know it's my birthday soon?" she quizzed, a puzzled look on her face.

"Aha, my dear, I have asked questions," Giovanni replied with a twinkle in his eye.

"All right, I'd like to spend more time with you." Emilia agreed to his request, and a soft pink blush coloured her cheeks. Shuffling their way down the crowded aisle of the church, Emilia felt a small wrapped gift slide into her hand.

"Open it when you get home and think of me," Giovanni winked at her. She blushed again and was surprised at his boldness; she hadn't thought to give him a Christmas present. It wasn't necessarily embarrassing because they weren't officially a couple. She accepted the gift with thanks and anticipation.

While the family prepared their yuletide tradition of mulled wine and amoretti biscuits before they went to bed, Emilia tiptoed to the bedroom for some privacy. Giovanni had given her a wooden photo frame with a delicate hand-carved ivy pattern and included a note.

My dearest Emilia, it gave me much pleasure to think of you while I made this gift. I hope you like it. I want a photo of us to put in it, to keep forever. If you can, I'd like to meet you at the big rock near the corner of the piazza at the New Year's Eve bonfire. Giovanni

The tender note moved her, and her heart swelled with an understanding of the love and joy they would share. She didn't have any doubt that they'd have a special relationship in the future.

A week later, New Year's Eve arrived, and the whole town would gather at the Piazza Sant'Antonio to celebrate La Festa di San Silvestro. A huge bonfire would be built up in the open space beside the piazza where music, dancing, food and wine and a magnificent fireworks display at midnight was organised by the village municipality every year. There was a buzz of excitement in the air, even though it was cold and the sky darkened early. Young people, the elderly and parents with children of all ages looked forward to the event as another year was about to end with the hope and expectations of what a new year would bring.

Butterflies flitted around in Giovanni's stomach, nervous anticipation nibbled at the edge of his thoughts. What if she'd changed her mind? Would he embarrass himself in front of her? Maybe her father had already arranged for someone else to court his daughter. Just dance, he knew Emilia would dance until his feet ached and he could barely stand up any longer. That was it, get her dancing and then sit by the bonfire, a most romantic notion indeed.

Emilia fussed with her hair after pulling out the rollers she'd suffered on her head all day. Her dark hair was fine and flyaway, and if she didn't use the rollers a puff of wind could blow it out of place in a most unladylike manner. Each curl was combed into place, and a gossamer spray was used to hold it firm. She painstakingly coiffed her hair until she was satisfied with a job well done. The looking glass reflected a small face with wide-set hazel eyes, a slim nose and delicate lips. She needed a touch of colour on her face, so she used a little lipstick and blush, then dabbed some perfume on her pretty handkerchief, neck and wrists. She pulled her coat over the carefully selected dress and beads and tucked a warm scarf under her lapel.

Emilia was ready. Prepared for anything she thought, to grow up and dance the night away with her one true love.

"Oh dear," she thought aloud, "I haven't admitted that to myself before." But there it was – she was in love with Giovanni Nostrini. She was ready for all the things they would share, as well as the difficulties and decisions they would have to make together throughout the rest of their lives.

Yes, *she* was ready, and she hoped her Papa would be too – in thirteen days – to hear from her beloved and agree to his proposal. After all, at 17 she would be a grown woman. Some of her friends from the village were already married, not all were happy, but they'd make the best of it because that's what you did. At least I know I'll be loved, cherished and treated with respect, Emilia mused. Her Giovanni was a gentleman and kind, with an innate sense of responsibility. She was pleased to become a part of his life.

Mama, Papa, Emilia, Franca, Nino and Anna-Maria stepped out of the house into the street which was filling up with neighbours heading in the same direction towards the piazza. A soft glow from porch lights lit the path along the way. It was chilly outside, but soon they would warm themselves by the bonfire. Emilia's mind flooded with memories of this community tradition. She remembered being beside herself with excitement when she was a child, looking forward to the giant flames that reached up to the sky. Fierce yet heart-warming at the same time, it wasn't quite as overwhelming as an adult. However, a sense of wonder remained. This year she would share it with Giovanni, his first New Year's Eve in her town. Emilia wasn't sure if they had a similar celebration where he'd come from, but she knew most villages in the Valtellina had bonfires even if they didn't have fireworks. Thinking about him made her a little breathless, she was eager to see him again. It had been a week since their secret meeting at church.

As the family approached the piazza, Emilia looked around the crowd towards the rock Giovanni had mentioned but found it difficult to see him. She excused herself and wandered off, her heart just about jumped out of her chest when she noticed him standing there. He had one leg bent with his foot back on the rock and rested his arm on his knee. Giovanni was having a smoke, the only misgiving she had about him. As soon as he saw her, he put it out and smiled, then came forward to greet her. Emilia's heart melted as they looked deep into each other's eyes, and without saying a word, love radiated throughout their very being.

"*Buonasera*," his deep voice echoed her soft words at the same time, and they decided to walk, talk and have a snack from the food table. They enjoyed the festivities of the evening together. After the ceremonial lighting of the bonfire, Emilia and Giovanni danced until it was time for the midnight countdown to begin.

"*Deici, nove, otto, sette, sei, cinque, quattro, tre, due, uno!*" A chorus of "*Felice Anno Nuovo*" rang throughout the piazza. Giovanni planned to steal his first kiss from Emilia on this night because he could get away with it; it was New Year's Eve after all. He bent down and took the side of her face gently in his large hand, leant in and placed his lips on hers, a tender kiss, slow and meaningful. He longed to linger in the moment but didn't. Giovanni pulled back a little, looked into her eyes and whispered so only she could hear him.

"Happy New Year Emilia, this will be our year, yours and mine. I love you."

She tingled all over, flushed with joy because she hadn't even contemplated the possibility of a kiss. How lovely it was, oh my, she thought, don't stop – do it again. Oh dear, her thoughts had run away from her. Fortunately, they were interrupted by friends and neighbours who wanted hugs and kisses to celebrate the arrival of 1939. There were loud bangs and popping sounds, the smell of sulphur drifted down as splashes of red, green and gold sprays glittered in the night sky. Everyone delighted in the display of fireworks. The band struck up again, and they danced until Papa said it was time to go home.

CHAPTER THREE

Rumours of War

THE TRAIN SLOWED AS IT moved onto a pre-selected platform track toward Milano Centrale, one of Italy's largest train stations. This city was the centre of national and international links for industry and, more importantly, for the economy of the country. Giovanni turned in his seat and watched for a reaction from the passenger who sat beside him. Emilia tilted her head and looked at him with a sense of awe as they pulled in and stopped. She was amazed at the size of the station with its 21 platforms. Conductors and train drivers smoked cigarettes and talked while they waited for their next departure. People of all ages came and went, called out, purchased tickets and carried their heavy baggage on board trains going to different destinations. The noise was deafening, it was nothing like the quiet siding at home two hours away. The four companions collected their luggage from the rack above the seat and disembarked from the regional train.

Emilia, Franca and Nino appeared as children in a state of wonder when they walked through the terminal. The arches, marble floors and walls, inset murals and high ceilings glowed as soft natural light from outside shone through the curved glass skylights. It was an imposing structure built as a major landmark right in the heart of the capital of Lombardia, and aptly named the Cathedral of Movement by its designer Ulisse Stacchini.

"I'm so excited I can hardly breathe," Emilia commented to her sister as they stood outside their hotel room not far from the massive train station. Franca was sharing a room with her, and Giovanni and Nino were sharing a room further down the hallway.

"There are advantages of having to be a chaperone for you. I'm just as excited as you are, I can't believe the size of the train station. Mama and Papa said it was big, but I had no idea that was what they meant. It seems we've lived a sheltered life, my dear sister. There's a big wide world outside our village, and it starts here," Franca replied.

"Mm, my world's changed since Papa agreed to let Giovanni court me; this last month has been like a dream. Who'd have thought we'd travel to Milano to go to the cinema? I still can't believe our parents agreed to let us come."

Emilia's conversation was interrupted by their trusted escort as he approached them in the hallway.

"Ladies, how about we freshen up and take a tram into the city for a meal before we go to the movie?"

"Sounds good, although I couldn't eat much with how I'm feeling at the moment," Emilia said, a mix of excitement and nerves fluttering in her stomach.

"You'll be fine. I'm sure the cafe will have something to tempt you. Even just a nibble from the antipasto," Giovanni smiled at her and rested his hand on her shoulder. She felt a lovely buzz run through her at his touch, relaxing the tension mounting in her neck and shoulders.

"We'll be ready shortly Giovanni," Franca nudged Emilia, "just as soon as I can get my sister prettied up without too much fuss," she winked and turned the key in the lock to their room.

After the jostling yellow tram ride to the Duomo, taking in the sight of elegant buildings and hearing the sounds of the city, they wandered into the piazza to the breathtaking view of a grand white marble cathedral. It was nicknamed 'The Wedding Cake', for all of its carved filigree decoration and 135 spires. The girls were agog with the stylish tailored clothing in shop fronts and fancy shoes on display in store windows. A huge poster claimed Salvatore Ferragamo's creations were, 'A sole for any walk in life – street, sports, evening'. The designs included his new platform and wedge-style heels. Since Benito Mussolini had invaded Ethiopia, rubber and leather were not available for shoemaking. Salvatore used Sardinian cork with fabric, lace and raffia as coverings instead of the traditional products.

They found a cafe nearby and ordered their meal. It was a novelty to eat out and watch the people around them. A photographer came into the restaurant and offered to take their photo. He promised to have it delivered to their hotel in the morning. The four of them posed by the fireplace, and another picture was taken of just Emilia and Giovanni together. After they finished their food, they boarded the tram to the Anteo Spazio Cinema for the opening night of the new movie, *'Ai Vostri, Signora'*, a comedy starring the famous actor Antonio Gadusio. They presented their tickets at the door, dated February 15, 1939 – Row J: Seats 17, 18, 19 and 20. The usher showed them to their row, and they took their places.

"Giovanni, I've never done anything like this before," Emilia commented, a little moisture filling her eyes. She was a bit emotional with all these new experiences. Giovanni took her hand, and placed it in his while they waited for the doors to close and the lights to dim.

"At your service, Madame," he stated dryly with a sheepish smile as he made the pun with the movie title. They all laughed at the antics in the film, with Nino appreciating the humour most of all.

The foursome returned to their hotel at the end of an entertaining evening, and after all the events of the day, they were ready for a good night's sleep. In the morning they went downstairs for their first hotel breakfast. The men read newspaper reports of the Italian dictator, Benito Mussolini's grand notions of rebuilding the Roman Empire to its former status. Speculation of troops to be sent to Albania and the North of Africa to achieve his desired political dominance was disturbing. He supported the Nationalists in Spain's civil war by supplying guns and ammunition together with Fascist Nazi Germany.

Giovanni had previously arranged a short meeting with his Uncle Peppino from Somma Lombardo. While they waited for him to come,

Giovanni insisted on taking Emilia back to the shoe store. Some of the styles were outlandish, but they bought a plain T-strap black velvet pair from the array for Emilia. She loved shoes and appreciated such an extravagance.

Zio Peppino arrived, and Giovanni introduced his uncle to Emilia and her family. They waited patiently while the men discussed the possibility of work in the near future. Giovanni could help build stoves at his uncle's business for a reasonable wage with only a small payment of money for board and food. Zia Chiara sent a message to say she was happy for him to join them and looked forward to seeing her nephew again. Soon he would head back to his original hometown. It wasn't something to look forward to, but it was necessary.

The prospect of leaving his Emilia behind did not appeal to him, or her either, but they both knew it had to happen to be able to build a life together. The sooner he started, the sooner they could get married, and it would be worth the temporary separation.

Two weeks later saying goodbye was painful, they had grown close over the short time spent together getting to know each other. Emilia had tears streaming down her face and didn't care who saw her crying. Giovanni stiffened his frame after he released her from his arms and braced himself to enter the train carriage.

"I'll write to you every week, Emilia. We can make arrangements for you to come and visit me at Somma once I've settled in, and when I can I'll come back here for a weekend too. Take care, my love," Giovanni called from the window near his seat, waving as the train moved away from the platform.

"*Ciao...*" Emilia choked back sobs and waved goodbye with her pretty embroidered handkerchief. She waited until the train disappeared in the distance and she couldn't see him. Digging in her handbag, she took out the treasured frame with their photo in it and hugged it to her breast.

Initially, weeks went by slowly, but once the newly acquired pattern of living became normal, letters were written and with the occasional visit, soon six months had elapsed. During that time they looked forward to getting their mail and sharing the details of each other's life. No thought or happening was too trivial to write about, and they both enjoyed learning of their deepening feelings.

Emilia had braved going on the train by herself a few times. Giovanni met her at Milano Centrale, and then they travelled to his uncle and aunt's place together. After the weekend she would return home in the same manner, leaving Giovanni at Milano. It had become less stressful for Emilia over time. Milano and Somma Lombardo had become more familiar, and she wasn't afraid like she'd been the first time. Her confidence in herself had begun to grow a little. She took the connecting bus from Milano Centrale to the other station by herself and caught the train to Somma, alone, so as not to take Giovanni away from his work to meet her.

At last Giovanni planned his first trip back to Morbegno since leaving. He longed to see his family again and spend more time with Emilia. He worked six days a week for his Zio Pino, so it was only Saturday evening and Sunday morning that they saw each other when she visited him. He was going to be home from Friday morning until Sunday evening, a whole weekend to enjoy with his loved ones.

When he arrived at Milano Centrale there seemed to be an anxious atmosphere among the travellers as he strode across the platform to catch his train. He heard snippets of conversation around him, and became aware Germany had invaded Poland; it was September 1, 1939. There was no official declaration of war, but the Nazis had staged Polish attacks on German installations to justify their *blitzkrieg*, a lightning war, where they destroyed Polish Air Force planes before they could take flight. They bombed bridges and roads; troops and civilians were machine-gunned down without any warning. The Polish people were unable to defend themselves and were overrun by the Germans. The news travelled far and wide and, on his arrival in Morbegno, they too had received word of the conflict. Fear of another war unsettled all of Europe, the Great War – World War I – was supposed to have been the war to end all wars. The Versailles Treaty was ineffective, Hitler had ignored the agreement and taken back the Rhineland, Austria and Czechoslovakia.

Everyone pushed these thoughts aside for a while to enjoy their valuable time together. Giovanni and Emilia, with her brother and sisters, went for a stroll to the main piazza in town to catch up with friends and play bocce. They rolled large steel balls as close to the jack as possible, hoping to knock the opponent out of the way. Short black coffee with a nip of grappa was the order of the day from the local bar. Raphael was encouraged to bring out his piano accordion and play while they sang traditional songs to warm their hearts and soothe their minds.

Carla Negri, who was visiting from Sondrio, joined them and she met Emilia. Carla had taken a shine to Raphael, and her obvious flirting had caught his attention and they'd been making eyes at each other throughout the evening. Carla was a bit loud in her manner, and Emilia wasn't quite sure whether she admired her directness or considered it a tad offensive. However, she was likeable enough, and the two young women chatted over their coffee between songs and developed what seemed an unlikely friendship.

Emilia answered all of Carla's questions about Raphael. They'd grown up together, and their families had known each other for a long time. Raph escorted Carla home to her cousin's house with Emilia, Giovanni and Franca in tow as chaperones. Carla's black wavy hair bounced on her shoulders as she walked; her large dark eyes were set under perfect eyebrows, and a natural blush freshened her smooth olive skin. Carla was quite tall, Emilia noticed now they were standing instead of sitting at a table. She pushed aside her envious feelings and was pleased for Raphael that he seemed to have found his match.

On Sunday they all met again at Raph's parents' place for a delicious long lunch. Carla spent the morning making pizzoccheri; the traditional short flat ribbon buckwheat pasta served with garlic butter, cooked cabbage and boiled cubed potatoes mixed through with Valtellina cheeses. After the meal, as a distraction from the gloom hovering in the atmosphere, Giovanni decided to regale them with stories of his stove building efforts and the antics his cheeky uncle had pulled on him in his time at Somma Lombardo.

Later in the afternoon news reports announced an ultimatum was delivered to the German government by Great Britain and France demanding they remove their troops from Poland. They ignored the instruction, and the Allies declared war on Germany. From what Giovanni could make out, Il Duce, Benito Mussolini had not committed his country to take sides with either the Germans or the Allied forces. Mussolini was the leader of the National Fascist Party, everyone throughout Europe knew of his relationship with Hitler and his aspiration to be a world leader. No-one was sure as to what view he would take on this new situation. Giovanni didn't know what to expect in the future. He thought, hopefully, it would be quick and blow over without a great deal of loss of life. It was a disconcerting departure in the evening but, for the time being, everyone pushed thoughts of war aside, they didn't want to think about how it might affect them. Italy was still suffering from the Depression that followed World War I.

It wasn't long before life continued much as it had done and Emilia and Giovanni went to work to save for their future as husband and wife. Emilia got a job in a factory packing canned vegetables, and although the work was tedious, it was an income of sorts to help with their savings. One morning while standing at the preparation table Emilia felt quite unwell, several times she ran out to the toilet and was sick.

"Emilia, what's going on?" the supervisor followed her out after another quick exit.

"I'm sorry Mrs Romano, but I'm going to be...," her voice trailed off as she disappeared into the ladies room. Ugly noises came through the door.

"My goodness girl, you're as white as a ghost. What's wrong with you?" A stern look of condemnation made Emilia shudder. "Have you been..., oh no, you poor thing." Emilia had doubled over in excruciating pain and passed out on the floor.

"There, there. Here, sip some water. Not too much now, an ambulance is on its way."

"What happened?"

"You fainted, that's all."

The nurse arrived with the driver and plagued her with questions. Soon she was on her way to the hospital where they diagnosed the problem. She had acute appendicitis and was rushed into surgery to remove the infected organ before it ruptured. To make things worse, while she was at home recuperating, her cherished Nonna Nina passed away. Mama said she couldn't go to the funeral because she wasn't well enough. Emilia cried at home, alone.

Newspapers continued to report the actions of the Allies who were in the Mediterranean off Africa; Russia and Finland were in a defensive battle, and Canadian troops had arrived in Europe. In Italy, another Christmas and New Year came and went and Emilia's eighteenth birthday neared. An announcement was imminent; they were to become engaged with plans to marry in early autumn. It was an exciting time with ideas for their wedding and honeymoon and where they would live was often in their thoughts. Many letters were written and posted between the two villages.

CHAPTER FOUR

War Time

GIOVANNI'S PREVIOUS HOPE OF A speedy resolution to the conflict in Europe ten months earlier was shattered at midnight on Monday, June 10, 1940 when Mussolini declared Italy was at war with France and Great Britain. The dictator hadn't made himself popular with anyone in his delay of choosing a side to support in the conflict. Hitler considered him a cowardly nuisance, Italians in Britain were immediately interned and the President of the United States denounced Italy's actions as 'the hand that held the dagger had stabbed its neighbour in the back while they were already down'.

There was a call to arms. All the men who had previously been to military training camps were expected to report for duty. A team of officers arrived in Milano for the arrangement and dispersal of regiments from the north of Italy. Units were deployed immediately to the French-Italian border via Milano, Genoa and Torino. Uniforms, fur-lined coats and hats, boots and knapsacks were distributed to the men, and orders given to the troops. Where possible, mountain men were sent for duty in the Alps, they were used to the altitude and living in snowy conditions. Raphael and Giovanni coincidentally ended up in the same unit. Both young men took the opportunity to write to their sweethearts before leaving by train for Torino. Two days later, after checking the mail, Emilia received her letter.

Tuesday, June 11, 1940

My Dearest Emilia,

As you will have heard by now, Italy has entered the war, Raphael and I will both be dispatched to the 5th Mountain Division high in the Alps, and we're on our way to Torino. Please write to me c/- 1st Army Headquarters, Torino, where we'll be reserves until further notice. We'll only receive mail when they can deliver it to us. I don't want you to worry, although I understand how difficult that'll be because of the circumstances. It's a sad day, and I'm sorry it's come to this, and while I don't agree with Mussolini, I'm compelled to do my duty. Just know I will be as careful as possible, with you in my heart and on my mind every day.

I've already been allocated the job of cooking for our unit. Our Commander has agreed to give Raph and me our leave at the same time. He was my training officer when I was in naja; he knows me well because he used to slip into the kitchen quite often for a snack. I'll write and let you know when we can meet up at Somma like we've been doing, but I don't want you to travel on your own now. Raph would like you to come with Carla as well. I'm just writing a short note because our train leaves soon and I want to get this posted to you today. I don't know how often you'll get letters, but I'll write when I can. Please keep us in your prayers.

Your ever loving, Giovanni

The soldiers arrived at Torino Railway Station, air raid sirens wailed, and damage from bombing attacks by the British Royal Air Force was apparent. Clouds of dust hovered over the city, and people scrambled through the debris to find cover and a haven in the chaos.

A few days later, after loading their food rations, camping and climbing equipment, guns and munitions into a truck, they got on board and headed for the mountains along the French-Italian border.

Raphael and Giovanni glanced at each other, acknowledging their predicament. They had a job to do, and orders to follow even though the equipment for the task was inadequate and they had no heart for it. Rumour had it that the old World War I fortifications along the Alpine Line were well-manned by the French but the Italian Army numbers outweighed them significantly. Intelligence reports of how many French *ouvrage* stations there were and their exact locations wasn't available, making their mission even more ominous. The *ouvrages* were concrete-encased fortification points linked together by underground tunnels. The further west they headed, the worse the weather conditions became, slowing their progress. Not being able to reach their prescribed destination by vehicle, or on time, put them at a massive disadvantage. Raphael was sent with the rest of the unit to advance on foot using skis or snowshoes. Giovanni and a few others had to tie the food and equipment onto mules they'd taken as alternative transport, separating the soldiers from their food supply.

Raphael trudged on behind his commanding officer, they were nearing the border when a summer snow storm set in, obliterating their vision. Some of the soldiers put on gas masks to help make breathing more comfortable and to keep their faces covered. The men continued in spite of the awful weather, and they were uncertain of their exact location because the compass wouldn't work in the freezing conditions. Raph was near exhaustion point and felt like they were going around in circles when the snowfall slowed and the heavy cloud cover lifted. A sense of relief washed over him at the change in their circumstances. Maybe they could see if the compass would work now and use radio contact to establish their bearings to discover where they were, and where they should be going. In anticipation of a request to prepare setting up the radio, he shrugged off the equipment from his shoulders. As he did a loud gunshot echoed through the air, and he was thrown down onto the snowy slope with the officer in front falling upon him.

Reaching to his side, he felt a warm sticky sensation on his fingers. He was gasping for air; panic gripped him, and his heart beat a staccato rhythm as more gunshots rang out. Men were falling all around him. Trapped, snipers caught them in an ambush attacking them from a fortification they'd encountered after aimlessly wandering around in the poor visibility. Waiting for the rapid gunfire to ease, and with the cold and wet seeping through his uniform, Raph tried to move his legs. Afraid he'd been injured and terrified of being caught as a prisoner-of-war, he managed to wriggle free of the man who'd fallen on him protecting him from the sights of a sniper. The blood was from the officer killed in the attack. Many more bodies lay motionless, bright red rivulets from their fatal wounds contrasting vibrantly against the brilliant whiteness of the snow.

Careful not to be noticed, Raph and several others crawled on hands and knees with their equipment in tow through the deep snow in the opposite direction of the fortification where the attack took place. A nearby outcrop of snow-laden pine trees could provide them with adequate cover away from the ambush site. Even though there was a visible trail to follow they hoped the French would be occupied with recovery in the conflict zone and wouldn't bother with a chase. They regrouped and began their retreat down the mountain, skiing through the trees as quickly as possible to find their regiment camp and report the incident. The ugliness of the situation haunted the men who survived. Hundreds of lives were lost, and many suffered from frostbite.

Sitting in his flimsy tent surrounded by darkness and the wailing wind, and wearing his fur-lined coat, boots and cap with a canvas tarp wrapped around him to ward off the icy chill; Giovanni had never known such extreme cold. Futilely, he'd thought to jot some more lines to his beloved's letter commenced a few days earlier. He pondered the words he would add to his note as his mind wandered back to the valley and wondered what she was doing.

'I expect it's a lovely evening at home, with a touch of warmth that is sadly lacking high in the Alps. Everything here is covered in snow, and it's so cold, even though it's summer. I've been reminiscing about the special moments we've shared together, and that warms my heart. I'm missing you so much, and I can't wait until this operation is over or at an impasse and we can have a much-deserved break. I have no idea when it will be, and oh, how I'd love a good hot cup of coffee!'

His hands were shaking so much he decided it would have to wait. He could barely light the lamp let alone try to write words that would appear legible. There was no knowing how long they'd be caught up in this camp before they could move along, at least in advancing the exercise warmed up the blood and gave an element of relief. The blessing of being the cook meant he got to stay near a fire when preparing the food for his outfit. Finding dry firewood to light the campfire was difficult, sometimes they had to dig through the snow to locate a dead branch or tree trunk to dry out by the lit fire to keep it going. Stoking it through the night was rarely possible because there was insufficient fuel. Sometimes when a new battalion of personnel arrived, they brought an illicit bag or two of lignite with them, which made the job easier. At other times they had to eat cold provisions, which wasn't ideal but unavoidable.

Giovanni strapped on his snowshoes. While bending over, he sensed someone standing behind him, he turned to see an ashen Raph fiddling nervously with the button on his top left-hand jacket pocket.

"What is it Raph? Do you want to talk about it?" Raph nodded.

"I have something to ask you."

He waited a full minute before continuing his request.

"Um, this is going to sound silly, but if I get wounded or die in the next few days, would you get the little packet out of my pocket and return it to Carla for me?" Giovanni was sympathetic, recognising Raph's previous experience as the most probable source of his concern.

"Sure, but don't talk like that Raph, you don't want to go into this defeated before we start."

"I know. It's just, well, you know how Carla is, and I promised her I would always keep her lock of hair close to my heart. It sounds corny, but I'd want her to know I did what she asked, and I don't trust anyone else to understand except you." Giovanni suppressed a smile.

"Your secret is safe with me Raph, it would cause me great sadness, but I'd be honoured to do that for you." Emilia's image filled his mind as he thought 'but what if it's me instead?'

It was June 21, and General Guzzoni had ordered his Army and the Alpine Corps to begin an offensive attack through the Little St Bernard Pass. Giovanni and Raphael's contingent readied to participate in the push of a 35km battlefront immediately. They were assigned to take the town of Séez, and then push on to Bourg St Maurice to overcome the opposition in that area. This section of the alpine defensive line was weak because the French High Command had shuffled its forces further north to fight the Germans approaching the Rhône Valley. Mussolini wanted his men to take the French Riviera and Marseille before the Germans could claim victory and hand the zone over to the Italian kingdom as caretakers. He tried to save face before Hitler in spite of the losses he knew they would have to endure to achieve this end.

It was an intensely foggy day, and they'd been trudging across the mountain for hours. News filtered through to their new commanding officer that fierce fighting in the south on the Riviera had progressed in their favour. The French were retreating after stubborn resistance for many days. Menton, on the south-east coast near the Italian border, was severely damaged from consistent bombing. An Italian artillery train had gained access through La Mortola tunnel to support the assault with weapons and munitions which had, up to that time, been lacking. The troops had good news for a change, and it boosted their morale, the front line was encouraged as they continued their battle in the Alps. Tired, cold and hungry, the men rallied until they arrived in Séez where their perseverance paid off. Victorious in their endeavour, they took control of the small alpine town.

June 23, 1940

My dearest Emilia,

At last, we have some positive news to share; thankfully our units have won a battle along the Alpine Way, and also in the south-east of France. It's been a difficult time, but it seems this is a significant victory for the Italian army. I've included the previous pages I've been writing to you when I could over the past few days. Knowing your love and prayers are with me keeps me going. I'll get this note to the ambulance driver who's collecting mail to post on his return to the hospital in Torino with a contingent of injured soldiers. Fortunately, Raphael and I are safe, and although exhausted we are both well enough.

Your ever loving, Giovanni

At around the same time he wrote his letter, the French were in communication with German and Italian leaders to sign an armistice to allow the occupation of their land. A French delegation went to Rome to discuss terms in conjunction with an agreed armistice with Germany. On June 24, at Villa Incisa, the signing took place giving the Italian army control of a narrow 50km occupation zone on the French side of the border including Menton and its inhabitants. The troops and families in the area felt a sense of relief when the news of the French-Italian truce was announced. They would not be faced with more devastating death and destruction while the agreement between the parties held.

CHAPTER FIVE

Reunion

CARLA WAS BESIDE HERSELF WHILE Emilia sat quietly and appeared to listen, even though her thoughts were elsewhere. The young women were impatient for the company of their men. Emilia experienced a slight flutter of nervousness and assumed Carla was too, considering her incessant chatter, the constant hair flicking and arm waving in a much more effusive manner than was usual, even for her. Carla had come from Sondrio with another young woman travelling to meet her husband in Milano. At Morbegno, Emilia joined them in their passenger car so both the girls had complied with the request to come together. In some ways, Emilia felt they were more conspicuous with all of Carla's antics, but it was a source of comfort considering she hadn't left home for several weeks.

Handsome in their smart jackets and pantaloons with caps jauntily perched on their heads, Giovanni and Raphael grinned from ear to ear at the sight of their girlfriends. They greeted each other, and the two couples indulged in unhindered hugs and long kisses. Tears stained the girls' pretty faces at the relief of knowing they were all right. Hand-in-hand they walked along the platform to their favourite cafe which had managed to keep its doors open for business. Giovanni wanted another hot coffee while it was still available. They'd all catch the train to Somma Lombardo in an hours' time to stay with Zio Pino and Zia Chiara.

Emilia was surprised to see the changes in Milano. Ancient buildings reduced to piles of rubble, bombing debris needed clearing away and broken windows were boarded up. It changed the appearance and atmosphere of the city. Shifting her focus back to Giovanni, drinking in the very sight of him and being in his presence made all the anxiety of the past weeks drain away. She relished their time together. Carla and Raphael went off by themselves quite often during their visit. Emilia and Giovanni sought to maintain social propriety with their relatives as chaperones during the four days.

August 24, 1940

My Dearest Emilia,

I've been posted in Bardonecchia near the French border, and our accommodation is at Forte Bramafam. It's an impressive fortified structure with kilometres of underground tunnels running in several directions. Although it's isolated and sparsely furnished, it's quite comfortable. We noticed the change after living in a tent on the mountain. The disappointing part is our breaks will be rare, and for about a week or two at a time, as there's not enough fuel to transport us to and from Torino regularly.

The summer sun has melted a lot of the snow we experienced earlier in our regiment's campaign, and if I wasn't aware of a war raging to the north and west of us, I could imagine this to be an enjoyable climbing expedition. The wildflowers are blooming and making bright splashes of colour on the mountainside along the army built vehicle tracks.

We're adequately catered for and have enough provisions to feed both the army personnel and alpine regiment. I have a kitchen to cook the meals in, but I seem to be making a lot of soup lately. Ironically the Mess appears, to all intents and purposes, very civilised. We have chequered tablecloths with proper cutlery, glasses and plates. There are stools lined up on either side of the trestles. We found some red wine in barrels in the munitions store that we weren't expecting, so that's a bonus. It's much warmer outside than inside the stone building, and we eat in the courtyard while we can catch some sunshine, the officers eat in the dining room. Chocolate and cigarettes are available if you've got money to pay for it. However, I can't divulge the source of our supply.

We have to think of ideas to build up our muscles because keeping fit is important. Today after muster in the courtyard area there was a massive rope laid out, and we had a tug-of-war competition. We were all yelling but we noticed a fluffy white dog with dark ears yapping as if it was cheering for each team. Our guns were off to the side, propped up together, and in its enthusiasm the dog knocked one over and down they all went like a row of dominoes. Poor boy, he frightened himself and hid behind a stack of boxes until we coaxed him out with a bone. No-one knows where he came from, or who he belongs to, but he has decided to stay. We called him Bianco, and he enjoys the scraps he can glean from us while we're eating our meals. Everyone likes him.

On Sunday the priest from the church in the village makes the trek up the hairpin bend track to take mass for us. We have to make the most of the opportunity to participate because when the weather changes he won't be able to reach us very often. The local people from the village bring up sacks of fresh produce from their farms as well. We trade with what we have that they can't get for their families, things like farina and riso. It works well for us all.

Last week we had a group of Polish and German Jews come across the mountain making their way to Montegenèvre, which is in France near the border, south of here. They are thankful to Italians for protecting their people. Even though the Nazis expect us to hand them over, we won't do it. There are thousands of Jews taking refuge in the Italian controlled zone because they know they're safe. We've heard reports of appalling treatment of them in different parts of Europe. As if war isn't already bad enough, and then they kill these people because of their race and religion.

A resistance worker named Marcel, that's his code name, who speaks French, Italian and German led the families through the Alps. They'd been in hiding for some time near Lake Annecy but had to get away from there because the German army is making a push south toward Lyon and the Rhône River. They'd walked across the mountains travelling for a few hours from dawn in the early morning light and again late in the afternoon. Finding somewhere to hide during the middle of the day wasn't easy for them. The only place they could get food was at a safe house in Albertville and Modane. French people have taken considerable risk to help them. We made up a food package and put them in the back of an army truck going to Genoa through Cuneo for the last leg of their journey.

Oh, Emilia, when they pulled down the canvas flap one of the little girls started to scream in a high pitched wail like a wounded animal. It was very distressing for everyone, and it broke my heart. Her mother kept apologising because her daughter was terrified of the closed up dark space after all the awful experiences she'd endured. They rolled the canvas up a bit to let in some light and air but left it down far enough to keep them obscured from view. I can't imagine what they must've been through, and it was a good feeling to be able to help them.

I'm sorry I won't be able to visit you for a while, but please keep writing to me and tell me about everything you're doing. I love hearing your news, it makes me feel like I'm with you. I've just about worn out my other letters from reading and re-reading them. Take care and give my love to both of our families.

Your ever loving, Giovanni

Sitting on the top step in the warm afternoon sun, Emilia held Giovanni's letter in her hand. She swiped at another tear as it rolled down the side of her face. It just wasn't fair, we don't even want to be in this war. How is an 18-year-old girl head over heels in love supposed to feel with this forced separation? She was angry. Their plans were delayed again and who would know for how long. She stomped off to the river and sat on the stone retaining wall Giovanni had built and watched the fast flowing water as it tripped around the rocks in the riverbed. Mounting resentment grew in her heart. Emilia prayed God would forgive her bad attitude and she was comforted that at least he was in a safe place.

Those poor Jewish people were much worse off with not much hope for their loved ones in comparison to her situation. It was strange those details weren't censored, maybe it got missed by whoever was supposed to check the mail posted by the soldiers. Some of Giovanni's letters had a few lines blacked out so she couldn't read them.

She was going to write every day, even though there wasn't much to say, and would wait either patiently, or impatiently, as the case may be at times for his letters to come. She would look forward to seeing him when he could get leave and be a bit braver and more confident each time she took the journey to do so. Emilia was leaving the shell of the quiet, shy girl behind and emerging as a much stronger, more independent young woman while still being the lady ingrained in her very being. No wonder Giovanni was so taken with her, he saw her potential before she understood it for herself. These events were beginning to expose signs of courage buried within that would carry her through whatever challenges she would need to face in the future.

Carla rapped on the door gently at first, and when there was no response, she banged loudly hoping to rouse someone. Emilia opened the door to see a puffy red-eyed Carla standing on the doorstep. Shocked, she grabbed her hand and dragged her into the house.

"What's happened?" Emilia pressed her friend urgently, holding her hand to her throat expecting terrible news. Carla started crying again.

"Oh, Emilia, I need your help. I'm pregnant! What will I do?" Relief washed over Emilia; it was a new life, not the loss of life as she'd feared. Emilia smiled.

"Oh Carla, that's such good news."

"No, it's not! My parents will be angry and disappointed in me, how am I going to tell them? What's so good about that?"

"You're having Raph's baby, which is always going to be good news. He'll marry you as soon as he knows. Have you told him yet?" Carla shook her head.

"No, I've only just found out myself, and I'm terrified. Please help me." Emilia put her arm around her friend's waist to comfort her.

"Of course I'll help you, we're friends Carla, and I won't let you down."

Arrangements were put in place for Carla to visit with Emilia for a few weeks, and in that time they began to sew and knit some tiny baby garments. A message had been sent off to both Raphael and Giovanni in the hope a response would come quicker than some of the other mail they'd received, at times it was weeks after the letter had been posted.

The mail arrived on Thursday afternoon addressed to Carla in Morbegno with a marriage proposal and a civil service planned for three weeks time at the Court House Registry Office in Milano. Both men were given leave in the circumstances, and an excited Raphael couldn't wait to take Carla to be his bride. Emilia encouraged the mother-to-be to invite her parents but Carla wouldn't hear of it, she was too embarrassed and planned to go home after the ceremony to announce she was married. In her opinion, Carla thought that would get a better response, and even though they would figure it out, it was her preferred plan of action concerning the matter. That was that, and Carla was back to being her usual self although she was, without doubt, much more up and down with her emotions. It wasn't like Carla to plummet into the depths of gloom, but there were days when it took all of Emilia's effort to coax a smile out of her.

A bouquet made from the flowers they could glean out of the garden on the wedding day looked somewhat bedraggled after a two-hour train ride. Carla was a little wan and quiet by the time they reached their appointed destination. She did brighten up when she saw Raph and was pleased when he got down on one knee and proposed just before they went into the building. As attendants and witnesses, Emilia and Giovanni stood alongside their friends as they said vows to love and honour each other. They signed the legal documents, and it was sealed, a very quick ceremony.

"I'm glad we don't have to commit ourselves to each other like this," Emilia said quietly to Giovanni. They wanted their wedding to be a joyful time to express their love for each other. It was a rushed visit with a scant meal, and then they had to say goodbye. It was all much too short for their liking, but the men had to return to their posts. Giovanni promised Emilia he would be in touch soon with arrangements to meet again. The men returned to Torino while the girls got on the train to Morbegno. Carla was exhausted and in no fit state to go home. She stayed with Emilia for a few more days before returning to Sondrio to face her parents with her marriage announcement.

December 10, 1940

My Dearest Emilia,

I've been given leave for Christmas this year. I'll be back in Morbegno in two weeks time and have ten days leave which means I'll be home for the new year as well. I return to Bardonecchia on January 4, 1941, so, I won't be able to celebrate your nineteenth birthday with you. Who could believe so much has happened in the past two years?

We expected to be married by now, so I propose we discuss a marriage date with your parents before I leave this time. It doesn't have to be a fancy affair, which isn't possible in wartime anyway. I long to see your delicate face and to crush you in my arms but I promise not to break any ribs.

Your ever loving, Giovanni

Two weeks! But the letter was written ten days ago, and today was December 20, only four days to go. Emilia was buzzing with anticipation. She dashed off to let her Mama know Giovanni was coming. What could they find to make it more festive? Food was becoming scarcer with only essentials available using ration cards. However, they did have a chicken that had gone off the lay in the henhouse out the back. It looked like its days were numbered now. They'd been putting off the inevitable in the hope they might get one more egg. It was decided roast chicken and a few potatoes left from last year's crop were to be included on the menu. It would be a fitting meal to celebrate Giovanni's visit.

The two families decided to spend the day together to share their food supplies and make the most of the special occasion. Fewer trains were running now, and Giovanni's father would only need to perform his guard duties once on Christmas Day. What a bright prospect it was in Emilia's days of loneliness and with the cloud of war hanging over them.

As promised, Giovanni discussed with both sets of parents about a time when they could arrange to be married. It would seem delay was a continuing theme for them and they would have to wait until October before it could be possible.

CHAPTER SIX

1941

NEWSPAPERS REPORTED THE CATHEDRAL IN Genoa had a fortunate escape on February 9, 1941 when the city was bombed by the British battleship HMS Malaya. A 381mm armour-piercing shell was fired into the south-eastern corner of the nave where a soft landing failed to detonate the fuse. The shell just sat there, no threat and no damage to the centuries-old cathedral. On the same day, the harbour town of Livorno suffered a great deal of damage from an air raid attempting to inhibit naval movement supporting action in the Mediterranean Sea.

Carla delivered twins, Gina Maria and Antonio Raphael on April 16, 1941 in Sondrio. It was Raph's suggestion that encouraged his wife to give a daughter her mother's name or to name a son after her father, with no knowledge they would end up using both. Raphael was far away on an island in the Ionian Sea off the coast of Greece at the time his children were born. In February he'd been transferred from Bardonecchia along with many others to support the Italian army in the spring offensive against Albania on March 9, led by Mussolini himself. The battle only lasted for a week and was a failed attempt to overtake Greece. Troops were dispersed to various areas afterwards, and Raph was sent to join the 33rd Infantry Division Acqui on Cephalonia. This small Greek island accommodated 12,000 Italian soldiers and navy personnel along with 2,000 German soldiers.

It took several months before Raph received word he'd become a father. He was ecstatic and passed around cigars to his fellow soldiers to celebrate, then got out his piano accordion and played many Italian songs for his compatriots. Carla's letter told him she was well and her parents were supportive. They adored their grandchildren, and living with them made managing the care of two babies at the same time much more manageable.

On June 22, Germany declared war on the Soviet Union, breaking a previously agreed peace pact. To show solidarity with the Germans, Il Duce, Benito Mussolini ordered a contingent of the Italian Royal Army to prepare for the German invasion of the Soviet Union. On July 10, an Italian Expeditionary Corps was transported to the Russian front to offer their assistance. This action was Mussolini's attempt to appease himself to Hitler after the significant Albanian failure, but it fell flat, and the Fuhrer was not impressed.

The weather was cold this autumn with the prospect of a frigid winter to come. It was a chilly day in northern Italy on Wednesday, October 29 as Emilia dressed for her special occasion. They rugged up well to face the icy blast of the wind as it wound its way through the village. It was disappointing she couldn't have the wedding she'd always dreamed of as a young girl, but it didn't matter because she was to become Giovanni's wife at last. They arranged their marriage ceremony at the local church with the priest who had served there for many years, and he knew them quite well. Only members of the immediate family came along because it was a weekday. Emilia shivered from nervous anticipation in the cold building as she entered the church with her father. He walked her down the aisle and handed her over to her waiting betrothed. Giovanni had decided against getting married in uniform because there were already enough reminders of the war on their wedding day.

Her voice soft and shaky, Emilia repeated her vows.

"I, Emilia Assunta Del Barba take you Giovanni Nostrini to be my lawfully wedded husband. To have and to hold from this day forth;

for better or for worse, for richer, for poorer; in sickness and in health; to love and to cherish from this day forth until death we do part."

She gazed lovingly into Giovanni's eyes while he placed the gold wedding band on her left hand. Emilia struggled to push the wedding ring over Giovanni's knuckle, so he helped her, smiling at her determination to make sure it was on properly. They were pronounced husband and wife, and Giovanni kissed his bride. It was a heart-warming day in spite of the cold weather. They had their photograph taken at the studio and went off to celebrate with a simple pasta dish for lunch. The newlyweds made their farewells at home before they left to catch the train to Milano where they would have their honeymoon before Giovanni returned to Bardonecchia.

A huddle of passengers stood on the platform while they waited for the arrival of the train scheduled to leave Morbegno at 2.30pm. A gloved hand pushed through a window of a rustic dark green carriage and waved madly. Emilia heard her name called out by a familiar voice. Carla skipped down the steps to alight quickly and rushed over to her friend. She threw her arms around Emilia and hugged her, so glad she'd been able to wish her every blessing on their wedding day. The twins were carried down from the train by their Nonna, while Nonno followed along behind with the luggage. They'd all come to stay with Raphael's parents for a visit. It was such a loving greeting, and in some ways Emilia was disappointed they had to leave right now. Carla said she'd wait for her to come back before they returned to Sondrio and they could catch up with each other then.

The couple boarded the train and waved goodbye to Carla's family as it pulled away from the station. They made their way into the carriage and found their seats, by the time they stowed their luggage Emilia felt somewhat agitated and a bit warm. Giovanni surmised it was all the excitement that had upset her and she'd settle down in a little while. Emilia hadn't eaten much at lunchtime. Giovanni offered to get her a snack, but she didn't feel like eating at all. Her new husband was concerned, but he thought maybe it was nerves about the wedding night to come. However, she did look a little grey, and her eyes were a bit cloudy. He thought perhaps they should get a train in the city and go straight on to Somma Lombardo and stay with his family. Everything was familiar there, and Zia Chiara might be able to help out. They walked through the station at Milano Centrale towards the bus stop. Emilia found it hard to breathe and was sweating profusely. Giovanni noticed she was dreadfully anxious.

"Emilia, are you afraid?" Giovanni lifted her chin and looked into her eyes as he asked this in a quiet, sincere voice. Understanding his intended meaning, she replied quickly.

"What? No, no Giovanni. There is something very wrong." She started crying, "I'm sorry, it's supposed to be a special time for us to be together. Why is this happening? I don't want to get sick now. I had a sore throat last week, and I thought I was getting better." He comforted her and held her hand.

"It's all right; we'll find out what it is. Please don't worry." He took her straight to the hospital by which time Emilia was muttering gibberish and was quite delirious. As Giovanni leant across to try and keep her in the seat, he felt a sharp pain rush up his arm. Emilia had sunk her teeth into him and bit hard. Giovanni was embarrassed that the nurse witnessed this action, and he explained it was out of character for her. The nun asked a myriad of questions and checked her temperature which by then had soared to over 41.5°C.

The doctor was summoned. He marched towards them with a wheelchair, then commanded Emilia to sit in the seat and took her straight through to radiology for a chest x-ray. He examined her and explained to them both she was suffering from pneumonia and needed hospitalisation immediately. Giovanni didn't appreciate the attempts of humour to lighten the moment. The doctor suggested she was a fragile bride, and maybe he should just put her in a glass case and look at her. The nurse commented his wife probably wouldn't be able to have children now, and sadly it was too late for her to become a nun since she'd just got married. They were inane comments which annoyed him in his troubled state.

Giovanni waited until they took her away to telegraph his commanding officer at the Torino base and advise him of the situation. He also sent a message to her family and asked them to contact Carla at Raph's home to let her know Emilia was unwell.

His wife was going to be in the hospital for at least two weeks, and then she needed to be close to emergency care for a while afterwards. The doctor insisted she was too unwell to travel and Zia Chiara was happy to have Emilia stay with them to take care of her. His commanding officer agreed to accommodate whatever they decided would be best. So Giovanni went back to his posting and planned to return at Christmas to Somma Lombardo for a few weeks.

Five weeks later, early on a sleepy Sunday morning, on December 7, news of a surprise bombing attack by the Japanese on Pearl Harbour in Hawaii echoed throughout the world. Over 2,300 lives were lost, twelve ships sunk, and others severely damaged with 160 bombed aircraft and almost as many wrecked. On this day Japan and the United States of America entered World War II.

It was the coldest winter Europe had ever experienced. Freezing temperatures had most of the Alpine regiment and other soldiers on edge at the fort. There was little to do, little to eat and a lot of time to spend doing it. One could only play cards for so long before it became very dull, no-one felt like singing, and they were often buried beneath meters of snow drifts. Teaching the dog new tricks and playing with him kept them sane. The only work they had to do at Forte Bramafam was to dig away the piles of snow from the doorways and windows when the blizzards stopped.

Giovanni thought he would end up trapped in the Alps at Christmas, another disappointment for his wife. But an order came through for nearly all of the men to take leave, effective immediately, except for a skeleton crew of senior staff who were to remain behind until the weather cleared. A cheer rang through the cavernous arched hallways as the men ran to pack their gear. They looked forward to going away for an extended period. Fortunately, the officers had a soft spot for the men's mascot dog and volunteered to take care of Bianco throughout the remainder of the winter. The guides who delivered the message from Torino waited for the soldiers. They all skied their way out of the mountains to reach the transport point before they headed home.

CHAPTER SEVEN

Spring

GIOVANNI THREW HIS HEAVY ARMY knapsack over his shoulder and didn't wait for the train to stop before he jumped onto the platform. He smiled broadly. Emilia waited for him rugged up in the same smart woollen suit, hat and scarf she wore on their wedding day, but with a healthy glow on her face now. She'd recovered well after her illness. It was like a time warp except both of them were acutely aware of the wait they'd again been forced to endure. Giovanni dropped his pack and reached out for his girl. He picked up his wife and swung her around in the air as you would to delight a child. How she loved him, and how he loved her. They leant in and embraced each other, a smouldering passion ignited their senses. Holding hands, they left the platform and quickly traced their way through the back streets to the family apartment.

Polite greetings were made before they surreptitiously climbed the stairs. The warmth and glow of a lit candle set in a delicate spray of dried rosebuds and lavender scented the spare room. With the door closed behind them, they pushed aside all care for their privacy; tingling sensations ran through them. Alive with passion, they kissed each other fervently, fumbled with buttons, and sent clothes flying off in all directions. As Emilia and Giovanni discovered each other for the first time, they threw themselves on the carefully turned back bed and became one as a loud clanging sound filled the room.

"Zio Pino!" bellowed Giovanni. A great guffaw from downstairs drifted up as his uncle enjoyed the results of his practical joke.

"You are incorrigible. I wondered why you wanted to help me freshen up the room." Zia Chiara playfully hit her husband. The young couple looked at the underside of the bed to see three cowbells tied firmly to the struts of the frame, and they both burst into uncontrollable laughter.

As Giovanni was required to remain close to Milan, they decided to stay in Somma Lombardo until he received his orders. He helped his uncle make stoves, had fun retaliating with some practical jokes of his own and loved every minute of being with his wife each day. Christmas had been a meagre affair, and 1942 arrived without any fuss. A telegram was received by Giovanni to request his return to Bardonecchia.

The commanding officer invited Emilia to come along as well. She would be good company for his wife who was visiting the outpost. In January, Emilia turned 20. Fort Bramafam still didn't have a full contingent of soldiers because of the relentless winter cold and snow. Fortunately, their quarters were warm and dry. Most of their time was spent in conversation by an open fire with a glass of red wine, and a book to read or a pair of socks to knit. On the weekends a movie was shown to entertain them all. It had been months since Emilia had left her family on her wedding day, and she looked forward to going home to see them.

The grey-green paint on the walls looked a little shabby where the sunlight filtered through the lace curtain and lit up the old mahogany framed picture of the Madonna. It was all familiar but somewhat empty. She was on her own in the brass and enamel double bed, no husband, or sister to fill the space beside her. There was no little sister in the single bed against the wall either. Emilia looked around the room she'd grown up in and felt quite alone. Franca was away, and Nino had volunteered to train with the Tridentina Alpini Regiment a few weeks ago. Mama and Papa decided to shift Anna-Maria into Nino's old room, and for the first time in her own home, she had this bedroom to herself. They had thought it best for when Giovanni came home on leave so the married couple could have the bigger space for themselves.

Tears stung at the back of her eyes as the level of nausea rose to her throat again. Tiptoeing out to the toilet Emilia threw up for the third day in a row since she came back to Morbegno. 'Oh God, she pleaded silently, please don't let me be pregnant, and if I am, surely it would be better for you to take the child to be with you. I don't want to bring a baby into this world the way it is, nothing is like I'd ever hoped or imagined.' There was no doubt about it, she had to be with child. Dark thoughts of dreadful things she'd heard done by other women filled her mind. Knitting needles, bone hairpins, purgative salts, heavy physical work and hot baths were methods used to terminate pregnancies. Emilia shook off those awful thoughts, she could never attempt such things. 'Enough, no more self-pity', she straightened up to go and pretend all was well and put on the face she needed to show her parents.

June 1, 1942

Dear Giovanni,

I think I'm missing you much more than before we spent so much time together at Zio Pino's place and the Fort. It did feel like a honeymoon, and I treasure those memories. This week I went to see Dr Botta, and he confirmed my suspicion that we are having a baby. Other than the occasional bout of morning sickness I feel reasonably well.

I know you'll be pleased with the news that we're going to become parents, but I confess I'm gravely concerned for the welfare of this child. It grieves me that I only feel disappointment because we won't be able to provide adequately for it. The memory of my baby sister, Domenica, haunts me as well. She was only six months old when she suffered from pneumonia before she died. I'm sorry for being negative about it, and I hope you'll forgive me. It's difficult for me to manage the thoughts going around in my head without you beside me. I miss your encouragement and positive attitude about everything. I miss you so much.

Mama and Papa are thrilled about becoming grandparents, and I wouldn't dare let them know about my fears. They keep putting half of their food onto my plate to make sure I get enough to eat. Papa has pulled the baby carriage and cradle out of storage, and he's cleaning them up in anticipation of them being used for another child. I suppose there are days when some of his enthusiasm rubs off on me, and I can genuinely smile at the thought of our baby coming into the world.

We're enjoying the sunshine, it's slowly thawing our frozen bones after such a cold winter. We're growing a few vegetables from the seeds Papa saved last year in the hope we can get some fresh home-grown food. How I long for an insalata dressed in olive oil and vinegar. A bit like when all you wanted was a hot coffee, do you remember that? Maybe I have a craving? What do you think? Do you believe in those notions about pregnant women wanting to eat peculiar things at weird hours of the night?

Mama is knitting woollen garments for the baby because it will be due in January at the coldest time of the year. Carla has promised to pass on either girls or boys clothes depending on what we have. I hope we don't end up with twins, and I did ask the doctor if it was possible. He said there's only one heartbeat that he could hear at the moment. Please write soon, I'll be waiting to get your letter.

Love from your wife, Emilia

The envelope had obviously been sealed, opened and resealed when Giovanni received it, which concerned him, but he realised when he saw the postscript that Emilia had done it herself.

P.S. Giovanni, you will find this hard to believe, but Mama is having a baby too. She was wondering why she was feeling tired all the time, so she went to the doctor. Poor Mama nearly fainted when he said she was pregnant. Apparently, it's a 'change of life' baby. Now we'll have to share the baby things because she is due in November this year. Papa is in shock, and I'm not sure how I feel about it. There'll be no more putting extra food on my plate now. I'm sure Mama will need it even more than me.

CHAPTER EIGHT

On the Battlefront

Her hand gently caressed her swollen belly. She sat down and put her puffy feet up on a rough-hewn wooden footstool. Emilia sighed and sipped her hot chamomile tea. The roasted acorn coffee substitute did not sit well on her sensitive stomach lately. Fortunately, the chamomile daisy bush had flowered prolifically last summer, and they'd dried a substantial stash of flowers to brew into the aromatic tea. The intensity of oils and health benefits increased with drying the herb, and she enjoyed the soothing effect it had on her frazzled body. It had been a long morning moving from her home to Giovanni's parents recently purchased grey stone house on the edge of town. The number of trips she'd made up and down the outside steps to her second-floor level had worn her out.

Cesare Nostrini had used his nest egg of cash to buy the house from a distraught widow who had lost her husband and sons in the war. The dear soul couldn't bear to stay where memories haunted her every day. Grief for the men who would never return plagued her and she moved in with her daughter's family. Money was scarce and could only be used for limited purchases unless it was spent on the black market where costs were exorbitant, and sometimes that was necessary to get by because food rations were restricted. There was an advantage of living in the country where you could grow seasonal fresh food until an army unit came through and confiscated it. The property had a plot for vegetables, and an established orchard, but being winter the trees were bare. The rickety shed out the back was stacked with chopped firewood and was obscured from the road by the closed dilapidated wooden doors.

Papa was playing bocce at the Osteria when Mama gave birth to a daughter in November. Mama wanted Nino to go and get him, but he refused. He wanted a brother, not another sister. He wasn't impressed with the arrival Giuliana at the time. Now their home was filled with baby cries and happy chortles. Flannel nightgowns and cotton nappies were draped throughout the house to dry by the weak fire. Franca had returned home, and Nino had left Italy. Father Nostrini offered a whole apartment level of his newly acquired building to Emilia, and she was hard pressed to refuse the opportunity to create a home for her own family. Silvia was a caring mother-in-law, and it was an easy choice to make. Giovanni's letter welcomed the idea.

Fortunately, the widow had left most of her furniture in the house. The bed, kitchenette, table, and chairs had been dragged upstairs for Emilia to use. She added a few personal items to the shelves and put her photo frame on the bedside table. Mama had given her some cooking utensils and crockery, but it still appeared rather bare. She took another deep breath, satisfied with having her own space. Emilia longed for her husband to come and fill it with his presence and strength of character. She missed him; loneliness and longing crumbled her resolve to keep positive like he'd asked her to do. Christmas and New Year had been dull and disappointing. She would be 21 in two days and had no desire to celebrate her milestone birthday.

Throughout the night in the strange apartment, Emilia constantly wondered where her brother was. They hadn't heard any news from him, or about him. An uneasy feeling kept nagging at her heartstrings for him, a foreboding sense for his safety was beginning to consume her. Rising early from her restless sleep, she prepared a little bit of breakfast and ate it in the quiet of her new home. Deciding to bundle up and go out into the cold she waddled her way down to the church where she knew it would be comforting to light a candle and pray.

As Emilia entered the cavernous church, dull morning light displayed a weak glimmer of colour through the stained glass windows. Emilia quietly approached the altar and lit three candles, one each for Giovanni, Nino, and Raphael. Even in her ungainly state she knelt on the prayer board clasping her hands together beseeching God to keep them safe. After a while, she wiped away the moisture dampening her eyelashes and struggled to stand up. On the way back to her new home she sensed the burden of her heart lifting. Her parents-in-law were expecting her for lunch. It was their first home that was not a railway flat, they had something to celebrate. She would not spoil this happy occasion for them by being miserable.

The vast snow-covered grassland stretched before them, an endless blanket of white. Four Alpini Divisions marched in triple file to join the 6th German Army Division on the eastern front. The cold seeped through their boots, double woollen socks, greatcoats and fur hats into the very bone and marrow of each man. Hunger gnawed at their empty stomachs. They'd been trekking on foot for weeks after travelling by train to Berlin, then Warsaw and through to Lvov in the Ukraine. German, Hungarian and Romanian troops needed support on the River Don. The Italian Army at Mussolini's demand was deploying its Alpini Corps: including 2nd Tridentina, 3rd Julia, 4th Cuneense and 156th Vincenza Divisions. They all wondered at the logic of being sent to the Russian steppe when they'd been trained in mountaineering skills and warfare. The extra weight of the unnecessary equipment of hobnail boots, ice pick and ropes became a heavy burden to bear. It made no sense to Nino; he couldn't feel his hands or feet and was troubled that frostbite could cause him to lose fingers or toes. He endeavoured to move them inside his gloves and boots while he walked, willing them to warm up. He awkwardly pulled his woollen scarf back over his nose leaving just enough room to see where he was going. Nino allowed a beard and moustache to grow to keep his face warm. Some of the men were still smooth-skinned youths, unable to wear the cover of facial hair. The soldiers swapped positions in the column regularly to create a windbreak of sorts, allowing the person in the middle of the column an element of protection for a little while. These young men, many only 19, like Nino, had begun to form solid friendships.

Not being able to sleep or get comfortable Emilia got up and walked around pushing her hands into the small of her back. It was still aching even after having rested for some time. Her thoughts wandered again to Nino, and she sent up another prayer for his safety and well-being. She was due to have her baby any day now, and growing anxiety at facing the birth without Giovanni weighed her down. Maybe she should be praying for herself as well. She'd endured listening to many tales shared by the older women in the village about childbirth which had left her feeling mildly unsettled. Mama didn't have any problem with birthing her sister, even at her age, and Giovanni's mother was available to help support her. The midwife had checked on her every other day and indicated everything was normal. She didn't know how many times the pregnant young woman had thought it would better for her baby not to be born at all.

Emilia was up early scrubbing at the kitchen bench because she didn't have the energy to do it the day before and she wanted to be sure everything was properly clean. A sudden dousing of water ran down her legs and over her shoes making a puddle on the floor. She realised her water had broken but decided to finish off the job she'd started, and then clean up the mess. Emilia changed her clothes and went downstairs to let her mother-in-law know the baby was on its way. The labour was long and painful, and her Mama kept reminding her first babies were often slow in coming. She was tired and uncomfortable.

The contractions had been five minutes apart for nearly seven hours, getting stronger and longer as time went on. The midwife had been an hour ago to check on her progress, and she was only a good two finger-width dilated. Not enough to deliver her baby yet.

Silvia had taken turns to care for Emilia throughout the day. Rosa had gone home to feed Giuliana and reassure Franca and Anna-Maria their sister was going to be all right. She set them the task of getting meals ready for the family to keep them busy. Rosa returned and sat beside her eldest daughter to wipe her brow with a cold cloth, and massage her lower back when she shifted position. Facing the next phase concerned Emilia, all she wanted was for the birth to be over. Silvia came back into the room with a surprise announcement. Giovanni had come to see his wife on her birthday and was excited to find she was in labour. Three hours later, shaking and shivering, Emilia felt sick and exhausted. The midwife returned and encouraged her to walk around to stimulate the process. Finally, she reached full dilation. It was time to push, but Emilia didn't have the strength to do it, and the contractions had slowed down and almost stopped. She just wanted to go to sleep and never wake up.

"Mama", she whispered hoarsely, "I can't do this, and I don't even want to. Tell Giovanni I'm sorry." The midwife indicated to Rosa to come outside the room, leaving Silvia to care for Emilia.

"She has to co-operate Rosa. We need to move her into action, or we're going to lose the baby, and we could lose her as well."

Stricken by this news, Mama marched into the room with resolve. She, Silvia, and the midwife stirred Emilia roughly to compel her to deliver her baby. Giovanni sat outside the room with his head in his hands, terrified he would lose the love of his life and their first child. He prayed for God's help to get them through this. He could hear Emilia's cries and the urgent voices of the three women willing his wife into more effort.

It went quiet, too quiet, but then he could hear some brisk activity. A weak cry came from the room. A little girl with a shock of black hair, her face blue from the stress of the birth, was whisked away to get her breathing and warmed up. A little fighter too stubborn to give in was wrapped up in a blanket and put into her mother's arms. Emilia opened her eyes and fell in love with her daughter; a bond never to be broken was born at that moment. Silvia slipped out of the room to let her son know they had a baby girl, and everything was all right. Relieved, Giovanni broke down and cried. He went into the room to see them, and tears began again when he held his daughter and kissed his wife.

"I'm pleased we've got a little girl. I love you so much, Happy 21ˢᵗ Birthday."

The midwife filled out the paperwork, Place: Morbegno, Italia; Date: January 13, 1943; Time: 18.15; Father: Giovanni Nostrini, Mother: Emilia Assunta Del Barba; Gender: Female; Name?

"What are you going to call your daughter, Emilia and Giovanni?" the midwife asked.

"Rosanna Nostrini," Emilia looked at her husband who nodded in agreement. Weak with emotion and physically drained she glanced at her Mama.

"After you, Mama, and Nonna Nina. Thank you for helping me get through this."

Even though Rosa knew it was tradition to name children after their grandparents, it was a special moment for her, and she would treasure it always. First time Zia's Franca and Anna-Maria came to meet their niece and give homemade gifts to the new parents for the baby.

The Red Army charged with fury on January 14, 1943. Operation Little Saturn wreaked havoc with four units attacking, encircling and destroying the German centre, right flank and Hungarian troops. The Julia and Cuneense Alpini stepped in and were annihilated. Part of Nino's group and the reserves withdrew and escaped the encirclement of the Russians. Of the 15,000 in the Tridentina Division who'd fought, only 4,250 survived. On January 26, General Luigi Reverberi commanded the remaining men while he stood on a Panza tank, as the sun was setting, "Tridentina forward!" upholding the Alpini motto 'none should pass through here', and he led them with the other remaining troops into a final assault.

Gathering in Podgornje, which was ablaze where the munitions dump had exploded, and the supply depot was on fire, they attempted to form columns to march out of the city. It was chaotic. Panicked people were everywhere with carts, mule trains, sledges and trucks rushing to get away. As they approached Skororyb, scouts from the Tirano Battalion limped toward them from the raging battle taking place in the village. The Alpini approached with care because they only had rifles, and were being picked off by soldiers hidden in some of the houses. Two Russian tanks advanced, and a German Panzer came to the Italians aid.

Although Nino and his Alpino mate, Renato, thought it didn't stand a chance, they watched the more agile Panzer charge towards larger, heavier Russian tanks. It fired a direct hit at one and then pursued the other. The Russians ran and gave the victory to the Alpini. They faced twenty clashes in the retreat before reaching Axis lines. Many soldiers were frostbitten, critically ill, and profoundly demoralised.

After tramping for days, their outfit made camp on the outskirts of Zaslaw in the Ukraine, near Lvov, on their march toward Poland. Nino and Renato had wandered into the woods to relieve themselves when they noticed a shallow grave of emaciated bodies thrown on top of each other. Uncovered men, women and children were frozen in time and place. The horrific sight of these innocent people with gunshot wounds through their heads made these characteristically strong men vomit. As they continued through the Polish countryside, a few starving women and children crept out of the shadows and begged for food. What little hard tack they had was given willingly to these bedraggled people bearing a tattered yellow Star of David on their threadbare clothing.

It had been near there in a makeshift field hospital that Nino, and other survivors, had their infected wounds and frostbite treated. For many, they had to endure the rough amputation of limbs. It had been a foul-smelling, poorly equipped post, and offered little relief to their deteriorating condition. Nino was grateful he'd come out of it relatively unscathed. His contingent was sent back to their original assignments, the remnant of Romanian and Hungarian soldiers headed south while the Italian groups continued west.

Spring approached, and the warmer weather began to thaw the countryside. On the outskirts of Krakow, everything appeared orderly as they marched through the city streets. No bomb damage or chaos was evident, and the citizens looked well-dressed and well-fed. The Fuhrer had pronounced Krakow the Capital of General Government for the Third Reich. Such a marked contrast disheartened the soldiers and Alpini Corps. Even as Allies they were treated with disdain, and considered inferior by the Nazi regime. Not that they particularly cared because in their eyes it wasn't their war. The Alpini empathised with the Russian people and their plight against the Germans. They weren't particularly troubled at the success of the Red Army following the battle at Nikolayeuka, other than the massive losses of their men who should never have been sent to the Don by Mussolini in the first place.

Raph lay on his back in the long grass, looking into the deep blue twilight sky and luminous stars overhead. It was magical. This place was stunning, surrounded by crystal clear aqua-blue water, golden sandy beaches with smooth white pebbles, olive trees and cypress on the hills. Cephalonia was paradise, except for the fact it was wartime. The locals had intensely disliked the Italian troops posted on their

Greek island, and it had taken a great deal of effort to alleviate their suspicious natures.

Each day was the same routine, get up early, run for a few kilometres through country lanes and uphill on gravel mule tracks. The soldiers went past old women wearing black mourning dresses, headscarves and aprons. The grandmothers snapped ripe lemons off the trees or picked vegetables from their garden plots. Then it was back to the barracks to wash up and shave, eat breakfast and go to the firing range for loading drills at the cannons assembled on the beach at Antisamos. Afternoons consisted of the midday rest time followed by a swim in the warm Ionian Sea lapping in gentle waves along the shoreline. Many of the Acqui 33rd had musical backgrounds; they played the mandolin, guitar, squeezebox, viola, and trumpet or bugle. And sing, singing they did with enthusiasm, and they had fantastic voices; choral and instrumental items were practised late in the afternoon. In the evenings they delivered a presentation in the town square. These performances were to build up relationships with local families. The Captain was a smart man and had weakened the stronghold of defiant hatred by working his way into the hearts of the locals through music. Friday night was dance night, and everyone was encouraged to participate, although reticent initially, most had succumbed to the enjoyable merriment. Others watched while tapping their feet under the table.

Tonight had been difficult for Raph, he'd escaped the crowd and found this secluded spot to nurse crushing feelings of loneliness and sorrow. His piano accordion lay on the ground beside him, untouched, he couldn't play tonight. It was his twins second birthday, April 16, and he hadn't even seen them yet. He sat up and reached for the jacket he'd placed beside his instrument. Raph dug into the pocket and pulled out two packets, and a well-worn photograph of Carla and their babies taken a year ago. Carefully he opened them to reveal tiny locks of hair. Raph gently stroked the baby-fine soft black hair of his children from their first haircut six months ago. He was missing so much. He wanted to be a family man and a loving husband to his Carla.

There were plenty of opportunities available for the men on the island if they wanted to purge their sexual frustrations, but Raph couldn't bear to be unfaithful to his delightful, unabashed and enticing wife. He didn't get to hug, kiss, bathe, or feed his Gina and Antonio. It was hard to believe they were two today, over 1,500 kilometres away, without ever knowing their papa. It grieved his heart, and longing wrenched at his soul. He fell asleep counting the stars, knowing that at least they could see the same constellations in the night sky.

After Carla tucked the blankets around her worn out children, she went back into the kitchen to clean up. It'd been a lovely celebration, a small cake each topped with their favourite colour candles, and they played games with a few friends. Mama helped her save some of their flour and butter rations for the past few weeks, with a few eggs and milk this week to be able to put together treats for the twins. They sang Happy Birthday, blew out the candles with gusto and enjoyed the pleasure of something special. Raph was probably playing in the band tonight. It was Friday, and he'd told her all about the things they did on the island in his letters. Carla didn't think it sounded much like a war zone, and she wondered if he'd thought about his son and daughter's birthday today.

Uncertainty rarely got to her, but tonight she longed for them to be a family, a real one, together, doing what families should be doing on their children's birthdays. A sudden urge to cry overcame her, and she dissolved into unbidden tears hoping Raph did still love her as she loved him. Carla stepped out onto the balcony to catch a breath of fresh air and glanced up at the sky, it was breezy and a bit cloudy tonight. As she went to turn in, a shooting star hurtled through the gap between the clouds and caught her attention. Maybe Raph saw it too over there in Greece, she hoped so.

CHAPTER NINE

Escape

THERE WAS A GENTLE TAP on the door, and she almost didn't hear it because she was feeding her daughter.

"Come in," she called out softly. The door partly opened and she expected to see her mother. A boot, and then a man in uniform came in with a smile beaming broadly across his face. Tears filled her eyes. "Giovanni!" Her exclamation made Rosanna turn her head, and distracted her from feeding.

"Hello little girl," Giovanni couldn't believe how much Rosanna had grown. He'd only been home for a one night visit on the day she was born. He bent down and tenderly embraced both mother and child. Emilia started to cry, and couldn't stop.

Are you all right?" she mumbled, questioning the reason for his unannounced arrival. "Has something happened to you?" The baby fussed and wanted the rest of her feed. Giovanni rose from where he knelt on the floor.

"I'm fine. Move over, my love, and make some room for me on the couch. I'll take her. Give me the feeder, and then snuggle up next to me so I can have both of my girls close. I've longed for this day to come." Emilia looked at Giovanni with a myriad of questions in her hazel eyes. "Sorry love, I'm only here for about ten days."

"Oh," Emilia stated flatly, saddened by the news. "I was hoping you'd come home for good. You fit in here perfectly, just like I thought you would." He looked around and noticed things he hadn't seen before.

"It's nice, you've done well. How have you been managing?" She shrugged.

"I tried to breastfeed her, Giovanni, but I wasn't any good at it. Mama tried to help me too, and she's still feeding Giuliana. Since I didn't have any success she shares her extra powdered milk rations with me, so I have enough to make the bottles to feed Rosanna."

Their conversation shifted backwards and forwards from all the things happening around them to what lay buried in each other's hearts. It was a precious time, and they didn't stop talking until long after baby Rosanna had fallen asleep in her Papa's arms. They tucked her up for her six-hour evening sleep, had a bite to eat, and being emotionally exhausted fell into bed cuddled in each other's arms. They woke to gurgles and bubble blowing at four o'clock in the morning. "Does she always wake up happy?" Giovanni asked. Emilia climbed out of bed to put the kettle on the stove.

"Mostly, but it doesn't last long. Usually by the time I'm ready to feed her, she's crying." She added some kindling to the fire, and it fanned into flame.

Well, well, little one. Papa will have to play with you this morning while Mama gets your milk ready," he stated with a sleepy smile in his voice as he picked Rosanna up.

"Don't you go spoiling her," Emilia commented. "Remember I'm the one who has to get her back into a routine when you leave." She didn't want to dwell on the fact Giovanni would be going to Montenegro soon. She pushed aside the gloom that threatened to swamp her and decided to enjoy him being with them for now.

They smiled and laughed at their daughter's cute antics while she was feeding and playing before putting her back in the cradle. Knowing Rosanna would sleep again for about three hours, and after being reassured it was all right to do so, Giovanni reached for his wife and made love to her with a burning passion.

Giovanni was pleased when his mother-in-law asked him to be Giuliana's godfather at her christening. The priest gathered the family around the central font in the baptistry and asked for the parents and godparents of baby Giuliana to step forward. After Giuliana's baptism, it was Rosanna's turn. The priest performed the ceremony with her parents requesting the grace of Christ for their daughter, accepting the responsibility of training her in the practice of the faith, and acknowledging their duty to bring her up to keep God's commandments as Christ taught by loving God, and our neighbour.

"Do you clearly understand what you are undertaking?" the priest asked.

"We do." Emilia and Giovanni responded together.

"My dear brothers and sisters, we now ask God to give this child new life in abundance through water and the Holy Spirit. Rosanna, I baptise you in the name of the Father, and of the Son, and of the Holy Spirit."

The priest rubbed the consecrated oil on her head and poured water from the fountain over her face. She didn't take too kindly to that experience. Her Papa lifted her into his arms, and she quieted immediately. Rosanna looked up and smiled at the face she'd come to know in the last few days.

"By God's gift through water and the Holy Spirit, we are reborn to everlasting life. In his goodness, we pray, continue to pour out blessings upon these your sons and daughters. Make them always, wherever they may be faithful members of your holy people and send peace upon all who are gathered here in Christ Jesus our Lord."

Peace did flood Emilia's heart, and contentment she hadn't known before settled in her mind. On the way out of the church, Giovanni looked over his shoulder and remembered the day they were married here. He wondered if he would ever return. No sense in thinking about what the future may hold, anything could happen to any of them. All too soon it was time for him to go back to Milano to catch the train to the east coast and then be transported across the Adriatic Sea with his outfit. When he collected his replenished kit bag, Giovanni managed to arrange for a supply of powdered milk, a sack of flour and a bag of rice to be sent to his wife in Morbegno.

The Italian soldiers were greeted by a clear blue sky, a pebble beach and palm trees swaying in a gentle breeze. They were enveloped in humidity as the boat docked at Herceg Novi on the coast of the Adriatic. Having never been by the sea, the tang of salt air and the smell of fresh fish assaulted Giovanni's senses. The company of men were divided into sections, and a group of twelve men disembarked while others were delivered to their posting in Tivat, another attractive port with lush green-clad mountains as a backdrop to the stone buildings lining the shore.

They continued through the protected Bay of Kotorska into the natural canal taking them to Kotor. Giovanni's experience in mess halls had him assigned to the food distribution centre. He hoisted his kit bag onto his shoulder and left the boat. The commandant led the Kotor group to their makeshift barracks. The scene before him was different, it was a small remote community nestled along the flat shoreline surrounded by bare, rugged black granite mountains rising straight up behind the town. The bay was a natural harbour with several Navy ships anchored in the deep water. The rest of the men were sent on to their camp allocations in Budvar and Bar.

Giovanni felt remarkably safe in this village, even though their brief was to support Operation Schwartz against the Montenegrin Partisans. The Italian government had paid and supplied the Chetniks with weapons, ammunition and food to fight against their own country's communist rebels. The threat of an Allied invasion caused the Germans a great deal of concern that these same men might turn against their recent masters. Now it was necessary to disarm them.

Fascist Italian soldiers were brutal in their fight against the Chetniks. Other men, less loyal to the cause, tended to ignore or deliberately thwart the demands of their instructions. They were entirely sick of the murder, and torture inflicted on those who tried to liberate their own country. It was outright slaughter, for every German soldier killed they hung a 100 Serbs, or 50 were shot for every wounded German. Giovanni noticed the haunted look on some of his countrymen's faces when they returned to Kotor. Their eyes reflected a hollow emptiness as they tried to make sense of the devastation they'd witnessed. Only loyalists to Hitler's cause appeared to be content with the results of their labour.

A wan Emilia heaved into the toilet again. Morning sickness had struck about six weeks after Giovanni had left. Not surprised, and nowhere near as concerned as she'd been when pregnant with Rosanna, she battled through the day to take care of her baby girl. Silvia had guessed her secret early because it was too obvious to hide, but they conspired not to let her Mama know yet. Rosanna was only five months old, and now there was another baby on its way.

There was still no news from Nino, no-one knew where he was, or what he was doing. Alarming reports about Alpini being wiped out at the Russian front, or taken as prisoners of war by the Red Army filtered through causing distress to families who had sons and husbands in the alpine band. The surviving troops marched through Prague in late May and were near the city of Munich in early June.

The climate of the war in Italy was on the brink of change, the Allies invaded Sicily in July and commenced their way toward Rome. Confusion and a significant sense of distrust were evident, plots and counterplots among the King, Il Duce, Pope, Marshal and Grand Council unsettled the balance of political power. However, the King and his non-Fascist Royal Army were still active. The Allies bombed Rome for two days, and then King Vittorio Emanuel III arranged for the dismissal and arrest of Mussolini. He appointed Marshal Badoglio as Prime Minister and commanded the Royal Army to continue to protect Italy. Italians rejoiced at the fall of Fascism, although there was an ugly battle still to come before it would be outlawed. Mussolini was kept under guard in Gran Sasso, Abruzzi. The Nazis suspected a possible alliance with the British without the leadership of Mussolini, and they poured troops into the north of Italy to strengthen their hold on the area.

The late August sunshine radiated warmth on Raph and Nunzio's bare backs while they enjoyed being in the clear salty water. Nunzio came from Lago di Como, and he'd been swimming every summer of his life. He noticed Raphael only ever waded in the shallows or wandered into the sea up to his thighs without plunging into the deeper water. Last week Nunzio decided to ask Raph if he would like to learn to swim. Raph swallowed his pride that his shortcoming had been discovered, and agreed to it. It was conditional, though, because it had to be when the others had their siesta or were busy with the female company in the nearby cove. He had progressed from being comfortably submerged in the water without fear of drowning to confidently floating on his back. Now Raph was using over-arm strokes and kicking his legs to swim short distances successfully. Even though he couldn't go far, he was getting the idea. Nunzio insisted it was a matter of practice, and so long as no-one was watching him, Raph was happy to keep trying. Sitting on the beach drying his hair with a towel, Raphael turned to his new friend.

"Nunzio. Thank you for doing this for me, even though we live quite close to Lago di Como we never went there for summer visits. I appreciate your help."

"My dear man, it's been a pleasure. You're a good student. I taught my son and daughter to swim the summer before the war began. They were just six and seven then. I hope they still remember those days and haven't forgotten the special times we had when things were a lot happier than now, hey. It's been years since I saw my family. Do you have children?" Raph told him about Carla, and the twins he'd never had the joy of meeting. Sadness enveloped them as they retreated into thoughts of their families so far away, and a profound longing gnawed at their hearts.

Nazi suspicions proved correct, and on September 8, an armistice between Italy and the Allies was signed. Two weeks later German paratroopers rescued Mussolini from the Gran Sasso Hotel and escorted him to a hideout in the north of Italy where he began to establish his new *Repubblica Sociale Italiana* Party. As a precaution, the Wehrmacht increased troops in areas where Italians outnumbered them in shared zones. However, no further reinforcements were sent to the island of Cephalonia.

Raphael and Nunzio awoke before dawn to a shrill whistle blow. The captain ordered them to pack their kit bags, bring their weapons and fall in for roll call in the piazza in 15 minutes.

"Is the war over?" Nunzio called out. He was left with an ambiguous statement.

"This one here is, leave everything else behind. *Pronto!*"

Unsure what he meant, and confused, the men scrambled off their canvas stretchers and got themselves sorted. They strode down the hill to the square in the village. The Captain paced while the roll call was taken, his expression was intensely grave. His group of men became more and more agitated as they watched him. He stood before them and began his address.

"Men, as you already know, the King of Italy has sacked Mussolini and appointed Marshal Badoglio as Prime Minister. Recently the government signed an armistice with the Allies. We have orders to regard the Germans as hostile, and we are not to give up our weapons. Negotiations between our General Gandin and the German Lieutenant Colonel Barge on Cephalonia have failed." The Captain paused, took a deep breath, and blew it out slowly before he continued.

"We now face the dilemma of making a choice. The German's have given us an ultimatum to continue fighting with them, handing over our arms peacefully, or, surrendering. If we opt to fight against them, they will consider us to be committing treason. Several of our Italian Blackshirt regiments have already given their allegiance to the Reich. If any of you want to join them, I give you the opportunity to go now!" All the men in Raph's outfit remained steadfast with no intention of going anywhere except under the leadership of their captain, whom they trusted implicitly. Silence filled the air as first light inched its way into the sky. A touch of pink painted the wispy clouds overhead, and it created a graphic contrast to the poignant and disturbing announcement: "Then we will not give up our arms, and we will defend ourselves," he stated loudly.

Forming a long double column, and marching toward Argostoli to support General Gandin, Raphael and Nunzio felt numb. They were not expecting this turn of events. The idyllic lifestyle had softened them into a passive passing of time rather than preparation for battle. On their approach to Sami, a plane flew over them with a leaflet drop – the printed message indicated Italian soldiers who surrendered would be shipped back to Italy. Continuing through the Agripidies Pass, Raphael was seriously considering this option because he wanted to go home.

They passed through a wooded area near the lagoon as they traversed toward their intended destination, the sound of a loud siren overhead pierced the quiet. A dive bombing Luftwaffe Stuka flew low over them dropping its cargo on Italian positions in the city where troops were amassing. They could hear loud explosions shattering bricks and tiles, and fire breaking out in the buildings. Fortunately, they were obscured from view by the dense tree cover above them. More planes, and more bombs. As they came around a bend in the track, the captain stopped and yelled out.

"Halt!

Raphael could not believe it, tears stung at the back of his eyes. He was aghast at the sight before him.

"Oh my dear God," he whispered. He and many others crossed themselves. The captain choked on the emotion he felt and gave orders to some of his men.

"Cut them down!"

Three Greek teenage boys, a silver-haired man and a young woman hung from the branches. A sign was tied around their neck saying 'We are Partisans and have shot at German troops' written in Italian and Greek. Their hands were tied behind their backs, and their clothes buzzed with flies where they had soiled themselves. The girl's dirty and torn dress revealed large bruises on her exposed skin which had been inflicted upon her before the hanging. Her haunted, vacant eyes were a fixed stare. Wooden boxes and stools had been kicked aside where the evil deeds had been orchestrated. Some of the men leant over into the bush retching, unable to be sick on their empty stomachs. The soldiers carefully laid the bodies in an olive tree orchard nearby and covered them with army blankets. The padre said a prayer over them and quoted some scripture.

"The Lord giveth, and the Lord taketh away; blessed be the name of the Lord. Rest in peace." The troops remained silent for a minute in honour of the victim's loyalty to Greece. Grief overwhelmed the Italian men, barely a dry eye among them.

Two kilometres from the main conflict area near the harbour a group of Greek Partisans stepped out of their hiding place and wanted to join their battalion. A silent nod from the captain confirmed to the leader his consent to their inclusion in his group. Fighting alongside these men, and fuelled with anger not previously felt, they strode out ready for a fight. A nearby school hall accommodating 600 Italian soldiers was under attack by a band of Germans. Raph's group, armed with rifles managed to pick off a few men toting machine guns. They heard the rat-a-tat mow down those inside the building. Screams and gunfire blended into another horrifying scene. The captain called his men into retreat and skirted the edge of town. At *Casetta Rossa*, the Red House, hundreds of officers were lined up in the courtyard and murdered. Shot down row by row. Two German landing craft approached the pier at Argostoli, Italian artillery officers ordered the remaining batteries to fire. It was a successful endeavour and wiped them out. However, several German boats sat in the harbour unharmed. Over 5,000 Italian soldiers were massacred in a week of battle on the small island.

"Nunzio, I'm going to surrender and get on a ship," Raph whispered to his friend in the dark as they walked together during the midnight watch over their campsite.

"I can't do this anymore. I don't care if anyone thinks I'm a coward. This conflict is already lost. The last of the ships will be loaded tomorrow, and I'll be on one of them."

While Nunzio understood Raph's choice, he didn't feel compelled to do the same; the captain had just bestowed an officer's commission on him. He needed to honour his commitment to his new position. After his shift, Raph put down his weapon, picked up his gear and went to shake hands with his friend. Nunzio would have none of it, he held him in a firm embrace and patted him hard on the back.

"It's been good to know you Raph, let's get together after the war. I want to meet your family, and I'd like to introduce you to my wife and children too."

As Raph headed to the pier, he saw a long line of downcast men boarding the German convoy. He held his head high and walked up the gangplank. An inner excitement wanted to boil over at the thought of putting his feet on Italian soil again, to breathlessly make love to Carla, and to finally meet his children. A smile played on his lips but casting a look back at the island, remembering the devastation he'd witnessed there in the past week, he was weighed down with sorrow knowing Nunzio was still there. It had a dampening effect on his euphoria. The convoy of ships loaded with 3,000 men steamed up and readied to leave. One by one they sailed through the Sea Mill passage past Platis Yalos, headed west, and turned north into the Ionian Sea toward Corfu and the Adriatic. It was here the treacherous announcement was made, they were not being repatriated to Italy but were being sent to German work camps. Raphael could not breathe, a panic attack began to overwhelm him. 'Oh no, what have I done?' slammed through his thoughts. The ship ahead of them was blown sky high when it hit a sea mine. The great vessel he was travelling in veered to avoid the carnage of the ship they'd been following. Now they'd hit a mine as well! A deafening roar and an explosion blasted them, and the ship listed tipping men and severed body parts into the sea. Raphael was sinking, gasping for air and taking in water. Propelling himself upwards through the murk of the usually crystal clear blue water, he broke through the surface to take a breath. Coughing and choking on thick smoke and fuel oil, and surrounded by dead bodies Raph tried to stay calm and tread water to keep afloat. He was thankful that he'd learnt to swim. He stretched out his arms to slide through the water away from the wreck when another explosion ripped through the remainder of the hulk behind him.

Shattered steel flew through the air and sliced across the waves. A large shard lodged itself in Raph's left shoulder, he was wracked with searing pain, and his arm was useless. Unable to use the over-arm stroke Nunzio had taught him, he kicked his legs hard and fast and balanced on his right side as he paddled with his good arm. Blood began to leach from his wound, and he became light-headed and weak. He struggled to stay afloat. Raph prayed, he prayed for himself and his family. After a while, he had no fight left in him and slowly drifted down surrounded by the warmth of a thermal ocean current. Thoughts of his home filled his mind. He placed his right hand over his heart and grasped the pocket of treasures held within. Raphael relaxed into the moment as his lungs filled with water until he passed out at the lack of oxygen in his body.

The captain, Nunzio, and the padre crossed the Drapano Bridge with their men close behind. They'd been captured and forced to march with other outfits under armed guard to a court-martial. Four officers at a time were charged with treason, announced guilty and shot. While a witness to this outrageous brutality, the captain had been commanded to sing. He swallowed hard past the lump and the dryness in his throat and through tears and torment began with the words and melody of Ave Maria. His voice caught at the declaration of thanksgiving for the lives of those who were slain in front of him. A chorus of male voices supported him, and in the strength of their song they continued through the lines where their lost souls turn to God for repentance and ask for peace.

Padre Ormato stood to one side, he prayed for and blessed these souls as they prepared to meet their maker. Many gave him a photo of their family, a favourite talisman or a much-loved letter from a wife or child in the hope he could return it to them one day. The executions continued, and the captain and General Gandin were next. As the General turned to line up with others, he wrenched off the Iron Cross he'd received for his contribution at the Russian front and threw it on the ground. At this, the firing squad aimed their guns and shot him in the back. The captain was also shot, his few men left wailed with grief and fell to the ground unable to stand up any longer. Nunzio lurched forward to reach the captain and remove his body from the pile. He was shot in both legs and was hit just below the knees. As they prepared to take aim and kill him, Padre Ormato stood in front of Nunzio with his hands outstretched and begged the Germans to stop.

At that moment a senior officer came to announce that, with proof, soldiers from the South Tyrol would be exempt from the court-martial. The padre continued his plea for a reprieve and the officer halted the proceedings to consult with his commander. Half an hour later of agonised waiting, he returned with an order for the executions to cease. The driver of a taxi used by the Wehrmacht as a transport vehicle had been an unwilling witness to these events. Nunzio was bleeding profusely and needed medical attention. The driver backed the taxi down the hill to help the padre. They wrapped Nunzio in a blanket and awkwardly loaded him into the back seat of the car.

"I know a safe place to take him, Padre," he whispered. Padre Ormato was unsure whether or not to trust the driver, but he had little choice. Only 37 Italians were left standing, and 20 soldiers were ordered to load the dead bodies onto rafts to be dumped out at sea. When they'd paddled the rafts offshore, they were blown up with the attending soldiers still on board. The Germans confiscated the items given to the padre and destroyed them leaving little behind of the 33rd Infantry Acqui Division.

Nunzio was unconscious on the drive up the winding road toward the castle near Peratata about seven kilometres from the city centre. The impenetrable ancient walls towered above them as they skirted around to a safe house in Kastro. A trained nurse lived there, and many injured Greek Partisans had been smuggled into her home to be treated and recuperate, right under the noses of Germans and Italians using the facilities in the fortress. A secret tunnel connected the safe house to the castle complex where a doctor received a pre-arranged signal when his services were required. While they waited for him to come, they removed the stained blanket and cleaned the blood away from Nunzio's wounds. His legs were a mess.

The driver held a rag dipped in chloroform over the patient's nose and mouth rendering him unconscious as the doctor removed the bullets. Competent medics worked to stem the bleeding and repair the wounds. One shot had partially damaged a kneecap, and it would cause problems in the future, but Nunzio was fortunate to be alive. The padre's boldness to stand between him and the firing squad saved his life.

The evidence of the atrocities that had taken place on his island home enraged the taxi driver. Broken bodies littered the city, and flaming pyres emitted a putrid stench of burning hair and human flesh. His heart broke at the scenes of utter wretchedness before him, but his spirit was stirred into an indomitable desire for revenge. He would continue to watch, listen and pass on much-needed information to his compatriots no matter what the cost might be.

Rivalry to destroy ports along the coast of the Adriatic by both the Germans and the Allies was rife. Towns and villages were marked territory, and airfields began to emerge in flat pastureland making the people who lived nearby nervous. Italian soldiers in the Balkans were not safe and had to escape, hide or surrender.

CHAPTER TEN

A Long Way to Go

THE FISHERMAN'S SACK SMELLED AWFUL and had seen better days, but it was strong enough to take the weight of canned food, ground maize and a water-filled canteen. Cigarettes and matches were wrapped in a folded blanket and stuffed on top of the secured load. The countdown had begun. Two more hours in the dark under the floor of the seaside shack, and it would be time for the fugitive to leave. A local fisherman, Filip, had become a friend over the short time they'd known each other, and he was willing to help him get to safety. Dressed in dungarees, rubber boots and a pullover with holes in it would serve as a good disguise. He pulled the woollen beanie down around his ears to keep warm, but it was nervous anticipation that made him feel chilled, and not the cold air coming off the sea.

The wooden fishing vessel was in need of a good scrub, and a fresh coat of blue and white paint. The small boat bobbed up and down on the gentle tide with a rope holding it fast to the upper level of the jetty. Filip went about his usual routine. The German guard changeover would occur in about five minutes. His hidden cargo in the crate on the cart would make a stealthy exit during the usual chatty exchange further down the dock. He could slip unnoticed beneath a tarp covered in fishing nets. Filip had set the disguise some time ago and managed several reconnaissance trips into the shipping channel to meet Italian fishermen from Brindisi.

Everything was set to go. A torch flashed across the length of the jetty, and Filip raised a hand in greeting. He opened the crate and left the door ajar, lit a cigarette and leant on the cart to obscure the view of the exit route. He took a deep draw and released the smoke into the crisp air, and watched it waft away. Cloud covered part of the pre-dawn half moon. He tapped three times. A shadow dropped low and crept inside the boat while Filip clattered gear on the other side creating a distraction until the movement under the tarp finally settled. He pushed the boat away from the dock, reached forward with the oars and pulled hard. It was with a sigh of relief that Filip set off into deeper water where the motor could be started. Once they were out of sight, he hauled back the cover and let a relieved Giovanni sit up.

Bari was closer than Brindisi, but Brindisi was less conspicuous, and the British had just stationed a command post at the port. Giovanni needed to leave Montenegro and return to Italia. There was no other escape route. He and Filip had planned this for more than two weeks. A dim light glittered in the dark, and both men held their breath knowing there was every chance it could be someone other than the arranged clandestine rendezvous. The two men had their heads down to concentrate on the baited lines, and even though they weren't in the correct zone for fishing, they made it appear as though they should be there. Two short blasts, a pause and another short blast indicated that Giovanni's transport had arrived. He shook hands with Filip, and thanked him profusely, gathered his things and climbed the ladder to board the trawler that would take him south.

On October 13, Italy declared war on Germany. Italian soldiers in Nazi-controlled areas were now the enemy and taken as prisoners-of-war and sent to work camps, or to repair railway lines and bridges. Nino and his Alpino mate Renato had been captured and sent to Dachau as political prisoners. The lazy guard who registered them on their arrival scoffed at the fact they'd carried their climbing gear to Russia and back. He suggested they could climb the barbed wire fence in their hobnail boots and added with a condescending grin on his face that he would shoot them if they attempted to escape. Nino had every intention of escaping but smiled naively at the guard to fool him into thinking he felt threatened by him.

The darkness overwhelmed him, and the dank mildewy aroma suffocated him. Grit got in his eyes, and it took all of his effort not to cough, or sneeze. The rustle of leaves where the guard edged near his hiding place made him break out in a cold sweat. He held his breath, there was no dog, thank God, or he would be discovered. Nino silently counted to allow sufficient time to ensure he would go undetected, then shook off the leafy cover, and recovered his equipment hidden nearby. He crept toward the base of the cliff, readied his rope and gained a solid foothold then heaved himself up off the ground to steadily climb the rocky outcrop. Near the peak, and breathless, Nino threw the rope to make a final stronghold, but missed. He tried again, this time it latched onto the boulder and held firm. As he hauled himself forward, his foot slipped which sent a tumble of loose stones down the face of the rock.

"Halt!" the guard had returned, a loud click sounded as the trigger was pulled ready to shoot the escapee above him. Gunpowder fired, emitting a wisp of grey smoke as the bullet propelled forward. It left the chamber of the gun, whistled toward Nino, and penetrated his backpack as he scrambled over the peak.

Anna-Maria sat bolt upright in her bed on the floor, and she was soaked to the skin in sweat. It seemed incredibly real, but it was just a dream. She'd begged Emilia to let her come and stay to play with her niece. Relenting after Anna-Maria's insistence that she wouldn't mind sleeping on a makeshift bed on the floor, Emilia agreed. They had a lovely time together even though there was only a little bit of risotto to share for dinner.

The sisters chatted for a long time before they said '*Buonanotte*'. It had been quite late, which was rare for Emilia these days because the nights always felt long on her own. Anna-Maria shook her sister awake and told her about the bad dream. Nino had been shot, and his backpack had a gaping hole in it. She was too scared to go back to sleep on the floor and climbed into bed beside Emilia.

"Rosa, I am going to see Cesare. My fob watch has stopped, and I want it fixed." Lorenzo had managed to keep the family heirloom hidden at the time Italians had been called on to give up their gold wedding rings and jewellery.

"I don't know how long I'll be, and if he's not at home, I'll go to the station to see if I can find him there."

"Lorenzo, can you send Anna-Maria home please?" Rosa asked her husband, who threw an 'I will' comment over his shoulder as he closed the door. Lorenzo didn't find anyone at the Nostrini home. He'd knocked on both doors, upstairs and downstairs, but there was no response. He headed off to the railway station sure he'd find Cesare there. Emilia's father-in-law had an aptitude and love for repairing clocks, watches and sewing machines. Lorenzo waited on the platform for a train to pull up at the siding. He was surprised to see an old decommissioned steam engine being used.

There was an immediate flurry as Fascist Blackshirts yelled at passengers to get off the train. Upset and terrified people swiftly alighted from the carriages; two elderly women struggled to get down the steps while an officer barked at them to hurry up, and gave one of them a push. Everyone was told to get their papers out to be checked, and the train was searched. Unfazed, the old women ignored the demands and headed for the toilets while the soldier was distracted. As they approached the door, Lorenzo noticed one of the women's shoes had a heel held together with a piece of twitched wire. He stared after them, the scarf looked familiar too.

"*Buon Dio,*" he whispered hoarsely, shaken to the core. The women had avoided the document check and slipped back onto the train when a cloud of steam from the engine engulfed the platform before pulling away.

Cesare commented many unscheduled trains arrived now, the timetable was useless, and he was called on duty at any time of the day, or night. He happily took the watch to repair it. Cesare noticed a disturbed look on Lorenzo's face, unable to read the expression that lingered in his eyes. They smouldered with anger, and the station guard suspected it was the drama of the Blackshirts on the platform. He saw more of these officers in Morbegno since the Allies had pushed the Nazis back and progressed northwards. He was used to it now but remembered how disconcerting it was initially.

Two days later Franca arrived home from Sondrio, she'd been away for over a week. She sat down with Mama and had a cup of lemon tea while she played a peek-a-boo game with Giuliana in the highchair beside her. Lorenzo walked in and saw her.

"Hello Papa," she greeted him and stood to hug him. He exploded with rage. "How dare you? How dare you put this family at risk?"

Mama was shocked at the outburst and started to interfere, but Lorenzo hushed her. Franca's face paled as she absorbed the accusation and tears filled her eyes.

"I know it was you on the train the other day. I'd repaired that shoe as best I could. If we got shoes from the ration consignment like we were supposed to you might have got away with it. But that wired heel was exactly how I mended it. You might have been in disguise, but I know it was you, Franca, so don't deny it. Who was it with you? What in heaven's name were you doing? Tell me the truth young lady or goodness knows I'll beat it out of you." Mama was distraught.

"Lorenzo, stop this right now. Franca has been in Sondrio working for the Red Cross rolling bandages for goodness sake." He turned to face his wife.

"I think you'll find she's been doing more than that Rosa. Tell us what you've been up to when you go off for a week or more Franca."

Giuliana started to cry because of all the yelling in her normally quiet household, but her Mama was in too much shock to notice. Franca quietly told her parents she could not speak of it, for it was better if they didn't know. This comment was too much for Lorenzo.

"You will speak of it and right now. I will not tolerate any more of this insolence Franca.

She nodded her head in response.

"All right, Papa." Giuliana was wailing loudly, and no-one noticed someone come in the back door and pick up the crying baby, her sobs soon reduced to hiccups.

"I was taking a British airman on the train to Milano to be collected by an underground group transporting escaped prisoners from Germany through to Livorno and Spain back to their own countries." Lorenzo was puzzled.

"But you were with an elderly woman. Where was the airman? Was that who the officers were looking for on the train? *Dio mio*, what have you done?" Silence reigned before Franca continued to explain.

"He was in disguise, nobody takes any notice of two old women Papa. We were safe, and he had false documents if we'd been forced to show them."

"*Dio mio*, are you saying you've done this before?"

"*Si, Papa.*" Lorenzo was about to rail at Franca when a voice from behind caught their attention.

"She's done well, don't be angry with her." Everyone turned, astonished to see an elderly man standing there with the quieted baby in his arms.

"Papa, their work is vitally important."

"Nino," screamed his mother recognising his voice. She took his face in both of her hands and looked at him carefully. The greying hair she could see up close was powdered, but his teeth were yellow. "What has happened to your teeth son?" Nino smiled in response.

"It's just part of the disguise Mama, it'll wear off in time."

Lorenzo and Franca stood there stunned, the family fell into an embrace that left them all crying and asking questions all at the same time.

"Hello my beloved family," he stated, hugging them back. "Before I tell you anything about myself, let me assure you, Papa, what Franca has done is essential to the freedom of our country. I managed to get home safely with help from a Swiss-Italian resistance group. It's risky, but she's been brave, and now I'm back I can do it for her instead. Franca doesn't need to be involved anymore if you insist she doesn't."

"What are you saying, Nino?" whispered his mother.

"I'm joining a *resistenza* group in Genoa, Mama." He paused and looked at the baby.

"I can't believe how much Giuliana has grown. She is such a big girl now," he said as he tickled her under the chin to coax a smile from her sad little face.

The Fall of Fascism

AN EAGER FRANCA RAN TO tell Emilia and Anna-Maria their brother was home. She explained about her escapades in more detail than she'd told her parents while they made a bottle of milk, and bundled Rosanna up to go out into the fresh night air.

Nino was astounded when Anna-Maria told him about her dream. He reached over to his backpack to show his family a burnt bullet hole in the canvas, and then pulled out his dented water canteen where the bullet had lodged in the distorted steel. It was uncanny, a vision rather than a dream. He explained how he, and his mate Renato, attempted their escape from their captors while they marched from Dachau to a work camp at Friedrichshafen near the borders of Switzerland and Austria.

It was risky, but they'd seen enough to decide they would rather die trying to escape than stay in the clutches of the Nazis. Before the war, they'd both been on climbing expeditions in the area and were reasonably familiar with the terrain. They still had their mountaineering gear because the guard at Dachau who registered them was too busy being sarcastic to confiscate their belongings. Nino slipped into the forest and looked back as a gunshot rang out. Renato fell heavily behind a truck on the side of the road. He didn't get up. Adrenaline pumped through Nino's veins urging him forward as fast as he could go. After two days of anxious hiking toward the mountain, he found himself better able to think clearly about his next steps.

Ever watchful and alert to the sounds around him, he was aware of a border patrol that passed by the foot of the cliff. He decided to monitor the guard who came through several times a day, but not always at the same time. Sometimes he had a German shepherd and at other times was without the dog. It was too difficult to attempt the climb in the dark. In the early hours of the morning, he hid himself with a covering of leaves and branches, just like in Anna-Maria's vision, and waited.

After the bullet hit his backpack, Nino rolled several metres down the other side of the ridge before coming to a stop at the base of a massive pine tree. The realisation he was unharmed made him sob, he was safe now, but his friend had died and given him the chance to get away unnoticed. Fortunately, resistance workers who kept vigil across the Swiss border area for escapees found and helped him. While he travelled in Switzerland, and through Italia, he had to be careful. Nino embraced his return to his family and hometown with a passion for defending them from the clutches of Fascism.

The telegram in Emilia's hand shook when she took it from an ashen Silvia. It'd been delivered downstairs, and the postman waited for her to acknowledge she'd received it.

"I don't want to know what it says," Emilia whispered, "surely he must be all right. I know he is I can feel it. I know it, Silvia, I know it."

Her hands were shaking as she opened the envelope: Giovanni Nostrini STOP Missing STOP Whereabouts unknown STOP, it read.

"Oh God, please let him be safe," Emilia prayed. At least he wasn't dead, as far as they knew. The two women held each other in a comforting embrace silently absorbing the information. Emilia had to sit down. Giovanni didn't even know he was going to be a father again because they hadn't heard from him since he first arrived in Montenegro.

Carla lay on the bed in her room and sobbed. The curtains were drawn, and it was as silent as an empty church in her apartment. The pain in her heart crushed her very being. Gina and Antonio were with her parents to give her the space she needed. The yellow piece of paper screwed up on the floor bore the news Raph was assumed drowned in the Ionian Sea. It was unbearable, her Raph, her beloved, gone forever.

Giovanni was bone weary. He struggled to get comfortable on the uneven ground where he attempted to sleep, but sleep wouldn't come. It had been weeks since he'd arrived in Brindisi and trekked along the coastline to head north. His body groaned with the physical punishment of travelling on foot, but his aim to reach home kept his spirits up, and a determination to be reunited with his family encouraged him to persevere. He made sure he stayed out of sight and chose less travelled tracks where elderly fishermen came and went. If for some reason he was unavoidably seen he would blend in and could catch fish from the beach to supplement his supplies.

The weather had been cool and often wet; sometimes he took shelter under large overhanging rocks, in a belt of trees or a cave near the shore. At times finding fresh water was difficult along the marshy coastal areas, and at dawn or dusk before curfew, he would slip into a village to collect a supply from a *fontana*. The further north Giovanni travelled the more deserters he saw. He didn't consider himself a deserter because he intended to report to his command in Milano.

King Vittorio Emanuel III and Prime Minister Badoglio had fled to the safety of the south, leaving the Royal Army without leadership. The army was in tatters, and Fascist RSI volunteers overtook the northern and central zones. The Germans under Field-Marshall Kesselring had been pushed back by General Montgomery and the Allies. Giovanni had avoided the conflict zones but seemed to follow the path of destruction in its wake. Bombing devastated the town of Foggia in Apulia where he'd gone inland on his way to Termoli. He was appalled to witness a thief looting the few belongings left intact in a damaged house and business.

Aircraft flew low over dozens of allied airfields between Bari and Termoli. Two Australian pilots had seen a sole wanderer from the air several days in a row. They bailed him up late one afternoon and communicated with him by sign language until they found an interpreter to translate their intentions. Giovanni was dragged into the mess hall for a decent meal, given soap and a towel for a shower and slept in a bed for the night. He felt refreshed and thankful and left the complex with more energy than he'd felt in some time.

A fresh November breeze blew across the harbour in Genoa, and the temperature had dropped significantly. Nino pulled his coat lapel up to keep warm while he clambered over rubble to the moderately damaged house at the end of the street. It was where he would be briefed for his role as a resistance worker, his enthusiasm mounted the closer he got to it. There were Germans everywhere from Milano to Genoa, which encouraged him all the more to support the Allies.

Three hours later Nino, codenamed '*Aquila*', left the house with another resistance worker to be transported to Cuneo. He had to choose a name of significance because they couldn't use their real names. Eagle was his choice. The others laughingly teased him he was the Short Toed Snake Eagle from the mountainous Piedmont region. The Eagle would be a protector to watch from the mountains and fight the serpent for his cause.

The rendezvous was planned for midnight. The lines were prepared, the dynamite was taped together and disguised - detonators were stored separately in a protective box. Mission Scorpion was designed to derail the goods train commandeered by the Nazis which took steel for gun production into the Torino factories late at night. Sabotage of conveyor belts and deliberately missing hardware had slowed the progress of the assembly lines, but they needed a more substantial effort to delay the manufacturing of enemy arms. A scattered band of five in the dense forest waited silently in their positions for the train to come through the tunnel to meet its demise. Nino's hands were slippery with sweat, and he shook with nervous energy.

"Come on *Aquila*," he whispered, "you have to do what needs to be done."

He wiped his hands on his dark trousers, and mentally pulled himself together while he watched and waited impatiently. There was the signal, one, two, three, quick torch flashes from the bridge and swiftly he slid down the bank to the railway line. After deftly inserting the detonators, he ran with a length of the line ready to ignite the fuse a reasonable distance from the bridge. He waited for the next signal to tell him the train was on its way, and there it was. Taking a deep breath, he struck the match and put the flame to the readied fuse. It burned brightly along the metal track. Nino raced back up the bank and headed into the forest. He ran fast and counted all the way, their band hoped above all hope they'd timed the blast correctly.

A rumble in the valley could be heard, iron-on-iron as the wheels turned on the rails, and then the explosion. A horrendous noise echoed upward with the sound of twisting metal, and the smell of smoke entered their nostrils. Intense heat radiated toward them. The group inched forward in the direction of the glowing light to see if they'd achieved their task well. The engine was on its side, burning brightly, with a mangled mess of carriages behind it. They waited for the all-clear from the group on the other side of the tracks who walked the length of the train to look for any guards who might have survived.

Aquila's first mission was accomplished but leaving behind the destruction, and a burning forest did not sit well on Nino's conscience. At least other civilians weren't harmed. He knew he could justify his actions after the atrocities he'd seen at the Russian front, in German concentration camps, and the shooting of his friend.

A blizzard was a possibility, and Giovanni's threadbare and worn out fisherman's clothing did nothing to keep him warm. He'd washed them many times in a secluded spot along a river and bathed while he waited for them to dry. Recently though, it had become too cold to do that, and he'd taken to wrapping his blanket around his shoulders while he walked. His supplies were low, and he was always hungry. The day began with a light snowfall, and he needed to find a more substantial shelter before sunset. He couldn't keep walking in this weather without the risk of getting pneumonia. Winter had set in, and it was only going to get worse.

A convoy of Allied soldiers on their way to Orsogna had pulled off the road to refuel their vehicles. Giovanni tentatively approached the group and was welcomed by an Italian speaking Canadian corporal. He was a driver of a transport truck who offered him cigarettes and several bars of chocolate. The corporal had been along this road many times and told Giovanni about a safe house on a farm about five kilometres up the road near Guardiagrele. He described a tree-lined track to follow, and which gate to open, then told him about the signal to look for when he got close. It would have a glass of red wine sitting on the front doorstep if it was safe to go in, and if it wasn't, the glass would be empty. There was a bunker behind the shed if he had to hide. The Canadian told him the Germans and Allied forces were in a fight for occupancy of the deep water harbour at Ortona and Pescara held by the RSI.

Giovanni hoped the safe house recommendation was trustworthy. He approached at around midday. There was a glass of almost frozen red wine on the step, a welcome invitation. Cautiously he rapped on the door and waited. A middle-aged woman with grey hair pulled back in a bun opened the door.

"Can I help you?" Giovanni wasn't quite sure what to say, but the warmth of the house and the aroma of cooking compelled him to be bold.

"I need some food and shelter, and a Canadian army truck driver said you could give me some. I would appreciate it." She smiled at him and called over her shoulder into the room.

"Nonno, you might be able to understand this dialect better than me. I'm sure you'd love some male company. *Entra, entra.*" Giovanni went into the humble home, and three little girls stared at him. Their young mother smiled.

Tears stung his eyes as he shared the family meal, farm produce saved from the summer season tasted delicious. These generous souls found some warm clothes for him, the little girls vying for his attention. There were various sized trousers, shirts, jumpers and jackets strewn across the room.

"This one Vanni, it's my favourite colour," said the five-year-old, who couldn't say his name properly.

"No, I like this one better," came from the older child while the three-year-old watched the scene unfold in front of her unsure of the strange man in their midst. The old man sat in a rocking chair in the corner and observed the goings-on with a twinkle in his eye. He and Giovanni enjoyed their banter as they decided on a new outfit for him. He was kitted out with a wool jacket, shirt and trousers, an old pair of boots that were in better condition than his own and two pairs of socks without holes in them. They packed the other clothes back into the large suitcase, and he sat down to discuss his options with the adults. A decision was made that he should stay because the weather and nearby conflict prevented him from travelling any further for the time being.

The rafters in the loft over the barn were low, and Giovanni had to be careful not to hit his head when he stood up. The thick stone walls and clay roof tiles were sturdy and watertight. The warmth from farm animals below rose up to create a cosy, although somewhat pungently aromatic atmosphere. Settling in the crude bedding on the hay-lined floor was comfortable compared to the rough nights he'd endured for weeks. During the night he often heard the scratching around of critters sharing his space in the loft.

The Canadian corporal called in on one of his runs to deliver more *riso* and *farina di mais* to the family. Pasta and bread prices had more than tripled since September and were unaffordable for most people. Giovanni agreed to take the opportunity to travel northward to another safe house in Cepagatti with him in several weeks time. It was Christmas Eve and the loneliness of the holy season would be less noticeable in the company of these kind people.

On Saturday, January 29, 1944 Cesare Nostrini was born. He was a small baby and an easier birth for Emilia, a delightful bundle of joy named after Giovanni's father. Rosanna was fascinated by her brother but didn't understand why he cried so much. Silvia was on hand to help out whenever needed. She was delighted to have her family close by and spend time with her one-year-old granddaughter while Emilia managed to feed Cesare.

On a sleepy Sunday afternoon, an aeroplane was heard flying low, much too low, it began spiralling down at speed. Families in Morbegno ran for cover. Cesare held his new grandson, and Emilia clutched Rosanna tightly as they ran down the stairs to the cellar. The explosion of the USAF aircraft as it went into the Adda River echoed through the town, fuel combusted on impact and threw out heat and flames. The pilots had ejected and parachuted to the north side of the river. Locals quickly ushered them into hiding, gave them clothes and food along with directions to Partisans who'd help them escape back to the airfield in Foggia before the RSI Fascists could find them.

Partisan clusters were building throughout the country and although of different creeds, tens of thousands of volunteers from all walks of life included: the Garibaldi Brigades, Socialists, Liberals, Party of Action members, Non-Fascist Communists and Christian Democrats. Escaped POW's from Europe, Britain and America joined their forces. They caused agitation, sabotage and obstruction of communication lines to disrupt the German's plans. Women acted as couriers and spies in strategic positions. They supported the network of safe houses for the wounded, escapees and storing guns. Battles in central areas continued, with detailed information of enemy movement acquired and passed on to the Allies. Supplies of food, clothing, arms and ammunition provided by Britain were parachuted into designated areas to support Partisan activity. Locals were encouraged to resist German occupation, which they did.

Cattle trucks were hooked onto the engine at Giulianova on the east coast. Cows, sheep and goats had been confiscated from farmers who had shepherded them down from the mountain areas at the beginning of winter. Germans needed the animals to boost their troop food supplies, and the train was leaving after dark. Undercover intelligence proved the train would stop to unload livestock at each of the major centres in Ancona, Rimini and Bologna.

Giovanni wore a black balaclava and dark clothing and carried a small knapsack with a few items in it. He'd been taken to the train station and hid where he could see the activity on the platform. The instructions on how to board the train without being seen ran through his mind. It was risky, but the train covered nearly 300 kilometres over two days and would move him closer to home much quicker than on foot. As the cattle car lurched forward, he dashed across the tracks and grabbed the door handles. He held on for dear life as the train began to speed up. Fortunately, air raid blackouts and dense cloud cover prevented him from being seen.

Hauling himself up onto the roof took a great deal of effort. Giovanni crawled toward the vent in the centre and dropped into the car through a barely detectable hatch. The animals calmed to his presence, and he quickly found the false panel against the end wall. It was accessible by pushing the centre panel up and pulling it forward. After stepping into the narrow space, Giovanni picked up the board with the inside handle, pushed inquisitive cows away from the opening, and returned it to its place. Holes drilled in the floor allowed fresh air to flow through making the stifling space bearable. He was used to the odour of animals after staying in several barns at safe houses, and it didn't bother him. Anyone who looked inside the cattle car would be unaware of the disguised transport niche regularly used by Partisans to shift people north and south.

Eventually, he fell asleep standing up as there wasn't enough room to lie down. At two main stations, the train had slowed and then jolted to a stop. Giovanni heard men's voices as they unloaded their share of the cargo, and he anxiously waited for the train to leave again. No-one discovered him, and he breathed a sigh of relief. The next time it began to slow down he had to be ready to disembark from the moving train. Before Imola Station there was a bridge over the river and on the bank after it, there was a safe place for his landing without inflicting too much injury.

Giovanni was nervous. He retraced his steps up to the roof of the cattle car and lay flat while the train moved across the rural landscape. This way he could see in plenty of time where he'd be able to make his departure. He gripped the handles again and waited. There was the river crossing, the train slowed, and he jumped and rolled onto the dirty snow while the train continued to move away from him. Relieved, he got up and checked his body for bleeding anywhere. A gash on the back of his hand was the only injury he could see, but he limped as he walked toward the tree line where he would be out of sight.

Blackshirt Fascists went from house to house searching for recruits. Any eighteen-year-old boys who didn't report to the muster on Saturday morning were to be flushed out. The Lonconi brothers didn't hesitate to carry out their duty as dedicated Fascist *Avanguardisti*. Arnoldo and Marciano took pride in wearing their uniforms, they had always attended the *Balilla* as children and worked their way up to a non-commissioned officer rank. Mussolini was their hero. They knew the young men in their town and those who avoided recruitment and threatened to burn down their houses if they didn't present themselves for duty. It didn't deter families in the Valtellina from attempting to hide their sons or grandsons. Many of these young men chose, in preference, to join the resistance. The Lonconi boys had taken great delight in setting fire to mountain huts to prevent them from being used as hideouts by Partisans. Smouldering houses along the Adda River and the shoreline of Lago di Como were evidence of where threats had been carried out. Some families were left homeless, and many lost their lives.

Nino was in Genoa. He'd been called in from the Cichero division in the hills to take on the role of a courier. The previous runner had been injured, and the team leader knew of *Aquila's* agility and stealth, valuable qualities needed for this task. His duty involved taking detailed information of Kesselring's German battle plan to an agent who would pass it on to the Allies by coded radio transmission.

Today was the fourth time he was making the delivery. He used a different alley each time and walking along the path by the buildings he sensed something wasn't quite right. A young woman stood outside an apartment near an open door holding an unlit cigarette. She looked Nino in the eye and as he went to walk past she jerked him inside, and quickly closed the door. He heard the clicking sound of boots tramping down the sidewalk, and voices yelling out, 'Where did he go?'

"Sorry about that, my name's Mimi. Here put this on, and hurry." Nino was alarmed when a Nazi greatcoat was thrown around his shoulders, and she clamped an officer's cap on his head. Doors along both sides of the streets were being opened and slammed shut; their doorknob turned, and at that moment Mimi threw her arms around him and began kissing Nino passionately. The door was thrown wide open.

The Blackshirt glared at them and grunted a snort of disgust at their behaviour, then stomped off to the next apartment. Quickly, and quietly, Mimi led him down the passage and through the back door. They climbed onto two pushbikes leaning against the wall outside and pedalled away from the scene before the searchers began to look behind buildings. Nino wasn't quite sure what was going on until the young woman explained.

"We suspected an informer set an ambush to catch you. We couldn't warn you because you'd already left, so we decided to carry out a rescue mission that wouldn't put anyone else at risk. It was close though, I must say."

"Thanks. You're very strong." Nino ventured to say 'for a girl' but pulled himself up in time. Young women in the Partisan groups were full of surprises.

"I've got brothers, a lot of them, and I had to learn to defend myself when I was growing up."

"Ah, that would explain it," he glanced across at her, "I quite liked the kiss."

"Me too," she winked at him. He smiled and followed her lead.

It was difficult to determine who to trust, at times even Fascists betrayed other Fascists and Partisans betrayed fellow Partisans. Aquila had been instructed to go into hiding for a while, and he went to Mimi's family home where they hid him for several months. Nino got to know them and appreciated their kindness and support. When the search for him cooled off, and the informant found, he resumed his Partisan activities.

He was near Piacenza, not far from the Lombardia border. Giovanni had gone from one mobile campsite to another through a network of resistance groups. He'd been astonished at how many Partisans there were throughout the country working against the Fascists. The British and Americans supported these brigades with supplies of food, guns and ammunition. Giovanni was given the code name *'Cucinare'* because he cooked for them in return for the help they gave him. Occasionally, he had to take up arms in a skirmish. He met *'Il Capitano'*, a well-known Partisan leader in the area. A secret code used between the groups validated Giovanni's allegiance.

After moving through the Apennines, they'd made camp for a few days to plan their next foray. A girl rushed into the small clearing. Her anxious eyes flitted from one man to the next until they rested on *'Il Capitano'*. He looked up, and as he approached her, she turned. He reached out and pulled at her long braid and began to unravel her hair. This action disturbed Giovanni, and he didn't like what he saw. None of the other men said anything.

"What do you think you're doing?" Giovanni snapped. The other man looked at him with disdain.

"She's a runner. There's a message hidden in here." He pulled a long thin strip of paper from the dark hair hanging down her back. Her duty done, the girl disappeared. The man squinted as he read the tiny print on the ribbon of paper.

"Your position compromised – Germans coming!"

Giovanni shoved the rest of the essential cooking items and food into the drawstring bag while the others gathered up their equipment. The men left the site and ran to the nearest escape route. *'Il Capitano'* led his men through the familiar tracks and trails of his childhood. They ran, single file, in unison. Broom saplings slapped them in the face, and painful breath heaved in Giovanni's lungs. Their leader came to a halt ahead of them and paused to decide which path to take. Giovanni leant back against a rock wall with his comrades beside him and wiped his forehead with his sleeve. They drew out their canteens and took a swig of water. The overhanging rock looked like the best place to shelter, but it was risky to stay there. The hum of German aircraft muttered in the distance, and then explosions were followed by machine-gun fire. They didn't expect a bombing raid. They needed somewhere to hide, but this was too obvious. Some decided to stay. Giovanni and *'Il Capitano'* crept along the rock wall and dashed for a deep tree line in the shadow of a mountain. The two resolute run-aways clawed their way into the darkness of a ravine and didn't move. A plane swooped over them, and then banked right and made another circuit over the area. The bombs fell on the rocky outcrop and bullets splintered oak trees and shattered the rocks in front of them. Giovanni and *'Il Capitano'* waited as the drone of the lone aircraft continued on its destructive path. They shook off the dirt and debris that covered them. They had to disregard regret for the loss of their group while they continued on their course to safety.

A civil war raged throughout the country concurrently with combat against the Allies initially, and then with the Germans. Giovanni witnessed horrific scenes. Cruelty he could never have imagined, the shootings and hangings wore on his soul and mind. Civilians and troops alike were starving, and no warmth throughout the winter months had steadily demoralised the soldiers. Partisans continued to receive Allied assistance with pinpointed parachute drops in prearranged zones. While these were only temporary fixes, they were essential to their ongoing success.

Piazzale Loreto in Milano harboured a dreadful scene, 15 Partisans hung from the roof of an Esso gas station in April. Locals renamed it the *Piazza Quindici Martiri* in honour of those who lost their lives. The Nazis had reprisal hangings and shootings regularly to deter Partisans from their scheming efforts to undermine the Reich, but all it did was encourage the people to wreak havoc upon their oppressors.

Finally, Giovanni reached Milano. The last leg of his journey was to take the civilian train to Morbegno, home. There was no command to report to and he'd adequately contributed to the Partisan movement. He had done enough. Asleep, tucked away in a hidden corner of the train station wrapped in his blanket, Giovanni was woken in the early hours of the morning by a shrill cry. In his sleepy demeanour, he wasn't sure what it was he'd heard, but there was an eerie familiarity about the incessant primal screech. Then he remembered the child, the Jewish child on the truck as it left Bardonecchia.

A prickling sensation ran through him as he crept toward the sound. He saw an armed Fascist slam his open hand on the closed door of a windowless wooden train car yelling, 'shut up, or I will shoot'. Giovanni was mortified. Jews! No, it couldn't be, but there was no mistaking it. The child's screams were stifled by a hand to smother the hideous sound before the train began moving away to its murderous destination. He knew who was in that carriage and he was overwhelmed with grief and unbearable sorrow. After their effort to assist the family to safety nearly three years ago, they'd eventually been caught. Clandestine transportation of Jewish people was carried out at Milano Centrale where the evil deed could not be detected by civilian observers. They were loaded into cars on the underground track and lifted up by an elevator platform to the main station.

Heavy-hearted, and with his false travel pass and ticket in his hand, Giovanni took a seat on the train to Morbegno. All joy of his homecoming erased, he spent the next two hours staring out the window feeling numb. When would this end? It couldn't come quick enough for him.

CHAPTER TWELVE

Celebrations

EMILIA WAS HANGING OUT THE washing in the early spring sunshine, relief from the confines of winter settling over her. Several rows of nappies were flapping in the light breeze with toddler and baby clothes sitting in the basket waiting for her to peg them out. Pausing, she considered her lot, two children under fifteen months old and the work seemingly endless, always feeling tired and with little nourishment she'd lost more weight. Even in her circumstances though, she was content, her biggest concern was for the welfare of her husband.

Every day she longed to hear from him, and every day prayed for his safety. Emilia watched their children while they slept and hoped they would all be together one day. A movement behind her caught her eye, and her thoughts becoming visible before her took her breath away. Unable to move, believing it a figment of her imagination, Giovanni approached her and took his wife in his arms and held her tight. Emilia broke down and cried her heart out until they heard Rosanna call.

"Mama, Mama." Silvia came out the back door.

"I'll see to her, Emilia, if you like." Then she saw them, and she released a huge sigh almost as though she'd been holding her breath for a very long time.

"You're back," she whispered, choking on her tears. "Oh, thank God you're safe."

It was pandemonium, children and adults all crying, embracing each other and Giovanni met his son Cesarino, little Cesare, the affectionate nickname given to him by his Nonno. Giovanni had already seen his father at the station for a few minutes before it was necessary for Cesare to resume his duties for the train's departure. A celebration at the family reunion that evening included Rosa, Lorenzo, Franca, Anna-Maria and Giuliana.

Cesare knew there was work at the hydro-electric plant across the river. It was damaged and needed repairs carried out. Most of the male population were involved in the war effort as Partisans, Fascists or held as prisoners-of-war somewhere. Many had died, and there were few men available to do the heavy tasks at home. Giovanni jumped at the chance and started immediately, riding a pushbike to and from work, pleased to have an income to support his family.

At her Mama and Papa's insistence, Carla arrived in Morbegno on the twins' third birthday to celebrate with Raph's parents. They'd become quite feeble since the loss of their only son, and Carla visited when she could, which wasn't very often. She discovered after they heard the news of the drowning that Raph had been a twin, his sister died at birth, but he never knew about her. To talk about those sorts of things just wasn't done. While Carla was there, she wanted the twins to play with Emilia's daughter, but Rosanna was on the couch with her right leg jammed in a wooden box. Carla was bouncing Cesarino on her knee.

"Emilia, what happened to Rosanna? And, I must say, you're looking well. You've got such a healthy glow about you. Have you found a tonic or something? I could use it myself." Emilia hesitated and took a sip of her lemon tea. She didn't want to hurt her friend when she told her the good news, knowing Raph was never going to return.

"Giovanni is home."

Carla was amazed to hear how he'd walked home such a long way by himself through a war zone.

"He was devastated when I told him Raph had been sent to Cephalonia. The last time he'd seen Raph was just before he went to

Albania. He'd heard about the tragedy on the island from others on his way north."

"And as for me looking healthy, no, I'm not pregnant" Emilia insisted, "I've told Giovanni we have to be very careful. Just the thought of morning sickness every day for weeks on end makes me shudder. Can you imagine lumbering around with two small children to take care of before the birth? And then I'd have to manage afterwards with only a little bit of sleep. No, I know I wouldn't cope. Besides we barely have enough food for our family as it is, let alone with another mouth to feed."

Carla smiled and assured Emilia she was pleased Giovanni had come home safe.

"I'm glad he was here last week because we had to rush Rosanna to the hospital in Milano. She fell and broke her leg, but they couldn't do anything with it because she's too young. They told us to make a box splint to keep it straight, and she's not allowed to use her leg until it heals."

"Poor little mite," Carla sympathised.

"I was upset to discover what had actually happened from my neighbour. Maria, Giovanni's sister, was too afraid to tell us about it. She's only 16 and knew it would upset us, so she decided not to say much. Rosanna had gone upstairs with her to make the bed, and she fell off the window sill she was sitting on. Her leg got caught on the pergola on the way down, and fortunately, it broke her fall; otherwise, it could have been much worse. Maria told me Rosanna had fallen over, but I didn't realise how bad it was. She was in so much pain Giovanni decided the injury must be worse than we first thought and she needed to see a doctor. By the time it heals, she's going to have to learn to walk again. But she's still with us, thankfully, and we'll manage while she convalesces. It's frustrating for her, but she's a good girl and does what we tell her." The young women enjoyed each other's company several times before Carla, Gina and Antonio returned to Sondrio.

Strikes in Torino by factory workers brought production lines to a halt. Over 600 arrests had been made, and several workers were deported to concentration camps. Hitler wanted the factories dismantled and re-erected in Germany where they couldn't be tampered with by Partisans. All the groups and brigades joined forces and became a part of the overarching National Liberation Committee. More strikes by workers in Genoa and Milano frustrated Nazi efforts and undermined their ability to arm their troops adequately. Battles were fought and won in Monte Cassino, Roma and through to Arrezzo. Fighting in Firenze continued until the German-held Gothic Line was broken through by the Allies in September.

Carla was having her hair cut by a friend. She watched as the scissors snipped away and the long lengths of hair fell to the floor. It was like a heavy weight lifting off her shoulders both physically and mentally, and she liked the finished look.

She popped into the village store to get some bread and salami for lunch before heading home. The shopkeeper commented a man had come in asking where he might find Carla Bartolucci and because old Marco didn't know she was in town he'd sent him to see her at her house.

"Who was it?" she asked, biting on her bottom lip. The old man didn't know and hadn't asked. A lump formed in her throat and she found it hard to swallow, confusion was clouding her thinking, could it be Raph? Surely not, she dropped everything and ran all the way home where she saw a man with a slight limp walking away from the house. It didn't look like Raph, but she couldn't help herself. She called out to him.

"Raphael." The man turned.

"Carla?" He looked at her and smiled.

"Sorry, I thought you were someone else."

"I knew Raph, though. It's nice to meet you."

Nunzio put out his hand to shake hers. Carla wasn't sure how to respond, disappointment crashed through her heart. Obviously, she must've held onto a thread of hope that maybe Raphael would come home one day, but it wasn't him. Nunzio gave her a moment with her thoughts then continued.

"We were together on Cephalonia and spent time on the beach at Antisamos before the massacre."

Carla cringed when she heard that word, but knew it to be the truth. Her love had gone forever. Breathless in her realisation, she inhaled and blew out a slow breath, and knew she couldn't let this man go without talking to him.

"Please, can you come in?"

"Certainly," he limped up the steps to her front door.

Several hours later when the sun began to set, Mama and Papa came in to invite them for dinner. Her parents had met the man earlier in the day and kept the children downstairs when they saw Carla return with him to the house. Old Marco had delivered the shopping she'd left behind in her hasty departure. Carla's stomach rumbled because she hadn't eaten since breakfast. She was emotionally drained from talking about Raph with his friend and hadn't given eating another thought. Nunzio accepted the invitation, but Carla noticed during the meal a shadow crossed his face each time he spoke to the children. It hadn't occurred to her to ask him about himself.

"I promised Raph I would meet his family one day," he explained as the adults sat at the table with a glass of wine after Gina and Antonio had gone to bed. "We were going to get to know each other after the war." He continued, telling them how he'd received the devastating news of the ships being blown up after his rescue from the firing squad. It took six months of nursing care to regain his health before he could return home. The expected limp was a nuisance and occasionally became painful, but he'd recovered well, physically at least.

"And, Nunzio, your family, how are they? Can we meet them too?" Carla ventured.

Sadness enveloped the pause before Nunzio answered huskily.

"My family are all gone. My wife, son, daughter, parents and my brothers-in-law were all killed." Heavy grief filled the room, "I returned to find our home burnt to the ground. They were hiding my wife's two youngest brothers from the Fascists and one evening while they were all asleep the whole perimeter of the house had been set alight. There was no way of escape, and they all perished in the fire. I was stunned when one of our elderly neighbours came across and told me the dreadful news." Tears slid down Nunzio's face as he recounted the horrific event, they sat motionless, sharing in the terror of the story.

"I couldn't bear to stay there. I tried working for the ferry on Lago di Como between Varenna, Mennagio and Bellagio but with the problem knee I often lost my balance and fell. The skipper asked me to leave because he needed a reliable worker and jobs are so scarce it wasn't fair on someone else who needed the money and could do the job properly, so I left. I wandered around the lake to different places but in the end, I just needed to get away from it all, so I came here to look for you."

A brief silence and then Carla's father slapped his hand down on the table, looking very proud of himself for his brilliant idea. Negri Wines had an excellent reputation in the district.

"Do you know how to use a pair of grape clippers?" Nunzio looked up confused as he responded.

"Yes, we had vines up on the hillside."

"Good, then you can pick grapes for me if you like. I need workers, the harvest is ready and if you need to stop and have a break for a while, you can. Some of the vines are difficult to reach, but you can go where it's safe for you to walk. There's a hut on the lower part of the hill, and you can stay there. I can't pay much money, but we can give you food and shelter."

This kindness was timely, and he couldn't refuse. They offered him a bed for the night and Nunzio retired exhausted but contented. He felt as though he had a chance of survival, of making a new life for himself and the opportunity to fill a need in someone else's life. The numbness in his heart had begun to thaw. Sharing his story and feeling the sorrow of his loss hurt but it was a necessary pain on the road to full recovery.

Christmas Day, and Emilia's long-awaited dream of their family being together, was a welcome gift. Little else mattered, not the lack of food or presents or cosy warmth, or any of those things that used to resemble past celebrations. Emilia and Giovanni enjoyed laughing and playing on the floor with their children until they needed to have a nap. Lovingly they tucked up the little ones and decided to hop into bed themselves to keep warm while it snowed outside. It was a pretty white Christmas promising hope of a future without war and the tragedy of all that came with it.

Nino spent the yuletide with Mimi and her family in Genoa. A cease-fire in Piedmont on December 25 meant it was possible to go to and from place to place in relative safety. A load of Partisans climbed on board the truck with open bottles of red wine, singing heartily to cheer their gloom away. Their group leader had permitted them to relax and enjoy themselves. They decided that's what they'd do because it would be back to the nasty business tomorrow.

The National Liberation Committee worked together to isolate and pull down the morale of German troops in northern Italy. Partisan successes were beginning to gain momentum. The Allies continued to push up, and the war in Europe was changing, no longer was the Third Reich a machine crushing its enemy with its sights set on dominance. Hitler could not cope with the strength and determination of his foe to win against the hideous war he'd started. On April 19, 1945 an insurrection by Partisans in Bologna attacked the Germans, and the city was liberated two days later. Within the next week, the war was won when the Allies prevailed.

Torino and Milano were liberated on April 25, and Genoa had 14,000 Germans and Fascists surrender on April 26 to the Partisans.

German vehicles crossing the border were allowed safe passage on the condition any Italians travelling with them were handed over. On April 27 at a checkpoint in Dongo on Lago di Como, the 52nd Garibaldi Brigade discovered a disguised Mussolini attempting to flee the country in an SS troop truck.

Benito Mussolini and his mistress, Claretta Petacci were arrested, executed and their bodies transported to Milano. They were hung upside down at the Esso Petrol Station in Piazzale Loreto along with 13 other Fascists as recompense for the 15 Partisan martyrs hung there the previous year.

Europe and the world over breathed a sigh of relief and celebrations abounded at the announcement, 'The war is over'.

Work on the crumbling cities began. A clean-up of debris, restoration of public transport and essential utilities became a priority. When the Allies finally arrived in Genoa in early May, they were astonished at the progress made under Partisan leadership. The war was over, but political and social upheaval would hang heavily on Italian society for years to come.

CHAPTER THIRTEEN

Departure

ON SATURDAY AFTERNOON EMILIA LEFT the children with Giovanni and went for a walk to get some fresh bread for dinner. A crowd had gathered in the village, hands over their mouths in shock, some wailed and shook their heads. Arnoldo and Marciano Lonconi had been lynched and left in full view of everyone who would pass by. Reprisal killings of Fascists had been heard of, but none had taken place in Morbegno until now. Emilia gagged at the unbearable sight and couldn't linger like some of the others did. Head down she walked quickly to the shop, made her purchase and hurried back past the same scene except she knew not to look this time. When she got home, she was upset.

"Giovanni, they've hung the Lonconi boys' right outside the school. It was horrible." Her hand pushed into her stomach. "And their poor parents, what a shocking way to lose your sons." Giovanni held Emilia in his arms and rubbed her back.

"I didn't have much to do with them," tears stung her eyes, "and I didn't like the things they did either, but to kill them like that is...," the sentence was left unfinished as she sobbed into her husband's shoulder. These young men had grown up with her, Marciano born on the same day. Giovanni listened sympathetically, unable to tell her of the horrors he had seen during his time in service and his trek home. Bitterness was a cruel master and revenge in the eyes of one caused pain in the soul of another.

Many men never returned home. Their bodies weren't given a proper burial and families were cheated of the chance to say a personal goodbye to their loved ones. Memorial services were held in the churches for men who served in the same battalions. Nino participated in the Tridentina Alpini remembrance service for those he served with on the Russian front.

Families who protected Allied servicemen were surprised to receive parcels from America, Australia, Canada, New Zealand or Great Britain with thanks for helping to save their lives. Medals were awarded to the brave, some posthumously to a family member. Partisans were recognised for their contribution to release Italia from a Fascist regime, to suspend the monarchy, and to create an independent republic.

Every day was difficult, and most people struggled to find sufficient work and money to provide even simple things like food and clothes. They prepared gardens in the spring to grow and harvest fresh vegetables which would supplement meal tables in summer and autumn. Life didn't have the shadow of war looming over it each day, but a sombre haze sat there that they were unable to lift from their lives.

It wasn't just physical needs but emotional grief too, particularly for the men who returned from the battlefield. People began to leave, emigrating to the United States, Great Britain and Argentina for a better life, to make more money and escape the brutal acts of wretchedness they'd been subjected to during the war and living under Fascism. The King abdicated in May 1946 and left the country by ship from Napoli. His son, Umberto II took on the kingship. However, a referendum held on June 2 to vote for retaining the monarchy or creating a republic was held. The monarchy was officially ousted, and the House of Savoy was no more, and a republic was declared. The new constitution ensured any future claims to restore the monarchy would not be possible.

On Sunday, November 10, 1946 Silvana Lorenza Nostrini was born. Emilia and Giovanni's third child was named after her grandparents from both sides of the family. Silvana was fairer than her siblings with brown hair and dark hazel eyes. Franca had met her match; she and Pierino Tacchini had courted and written to each other regularly throughout the latter part of the war years. They planned their wedding for the last day of November.

Giovanni cooked the reception dinner, and everyone enjoyed the family celebration. Giuliana was four years old when her sister married, she loved getting dressed up and had a large bow to wear in her hair. It was a happy occasion.

The Paris Peace Treaty signed in February 1947 outlined territories and war reparations. Italy owed a great deal of money to Yugoslavia, Greece, Albania, the Soviet Union and Ethiopia that put a financial burden upon an already floundering economy. A general election was held in 1948 with Communists and Christian Democrats the major parties. The United States assisted in helping Italians oppose the communists, Italian-Americans were encouraged to write to their relatives, and Frank Sinatra made a Voice of America radio broadcast supporting the Christian Democrats.

Alcide di Gasperi formed a new centre-right government when the Christian Democrats won a parliamentary majority. However, the struggle of the people continued. Unions held strikes, and factory workers were laid-off disrupting industry and farmers struggled in 1949, leaving massive numbers of unemployed and a nation without the ability to compete in world commerce. It painted a very dismal future for Italian families, and they began to leave the country in droves.

Giovanni came home from work early one weekday with an envelope of paperwork. He spread the documents over the table and began to fill out the forms. Emilia looked over his shoulder and was shocked at what she saw. They were emigration papers! Giovanni had decided enough was enough, he couldn't provide for his family adequately in this society. A new beginning in a new country with better opportunities was their only hope for survival.

"I can't believe you didn't even talk to me about this," Emilia's voice was raised, which rarely ever happened.

"I'm sorry love, but this is for the best," Giovanni responded. "Your Papa is happy to pay for my ticket, and when I get a job and have saved enough money, I'll send for you and the children."

Emilia was aghast; he had talked to her father and already made the arrangements. She was dumbfounded.

"And I'll be left alone, again." She stomped off to their bedroom and slammed the door. Giovanni heard her crying and went to her.

"Go away and leave me alone. I don't want to talk to you," Emilia mumbled through her sobs. He decided it was best to comply with her wishes and went back to the table to complete his application to the United States of America.

It was a chilly atmosphere in their home for several weeks. Emilia would not even look at Giovanni. She was hurt she'd been left out of the whole decision-making process. Her husband gave her time to absorb the shock and was disappointed he hadn't considered what his wife's reaction might be. Several months later, a rejection letter of his application came through. America had changed its immigration policy due to the massive influx of European migrants and flood of new applications. Unsure about what to do, Giovanni thought it smart to include his wife in the next phase of planning.

Anna-Maria became engaged. Her fiancé was immigrating to Argentina with the intention to do what Giovanni had planned. Antonio was due to leave from Genoa in two weeks time. Anna-Maria wanted to escape the mundane lifestyle young people were tired of and looked forward to a new beginning. She didn't mind being left behind for a time and encouraged her sister to view it as a positive thing to do. Giovanni considered Argentina, but the best option was to apply to Australia. He had the opportunity of sponsorship with an Italian family in Albany, on the south coast of Western Australia. He was sure it was the chance he'd been looking for. Although Emilia reluctantly agreed, her worst fear was of being apart from Giovanni after finally having their family together for a few years.

Arrangements were made, and a passport with a temporary visa and sponsorship approvals were all stamped and he'd made the payment of his passage on the ship '*Napoli*'. A ticket for one sat on the dresser. His journey would have to go via the west coast of Africa and around the Cape of Good Hope. It would be a long and rough voyage but unavoidable because the Suez Canal was still being cleared of wartime wreckage.

The trunk on the bedroom floor appeared to fill the whole room, but it was blurred by Emilia's tears as she packed the folded shirts, trousers and other items for Giovanni to take. She gently caressed the carved photo frame he'd made for her and then wrapped it in a soft towel to protect her treasured possession before she tucked it into the trunk. She wanted her husband to have it with him when he would be far away from her.

"I can't believe this is happening. You're going away again, without me." Her melancholy thoughts were spoken out loud to no apparent audience. "How will I cope, I don't want to do it, it's all too hard."

Giovanni had to keep working at the plant to earn as much money as possible before leaving. Arrangements had been made for the shopkeeper, Senore Formigalli, to run a tab for Emilia's needs at the store with assurance from Giovanni he would pay for it by overseas bank transfers.

The family gathered for a farewell meal, the last meal they would share together before he set off for Genoa and Australia. Everyone endeavoured to be happy and pleased for Giovanni, but they all knew they might not see him again. Emilia put on a happy face for the occasion, but her heart was breaking with unbelievable pain at the impending separation. The whole family posed for a photograph, an enduring memory for his parents and the others Giovanni would leave behind in Italy.

Cesare and Francesco escorted their son and brother to Genoa. It was a hard day to face, but an occasion neither would miss. Giovanni was their flesh and blood, and while they would've preferred him to stay, they understood his desire to provide more for Emilia and the children.

Part Two
Australia

CHAPTER FOURTEEN

A Sunburnt Country

A SLIVER OF FLAT LAND appeared on the horizon of the Indian Ocean. They said that was Australia. A tingle ran through Giovanni, finally, he was close to his destination. One last evening on the boat after nearly seven weeks at sea and he would be able to put his feet on dry land again. The passengers aboard the *'Napoli'* would not have been able to comprehend the vastness of the country they approached. Perth, the capital city of Western Australia, was nestled on the north and south sides of the Swan River. The river was tinged an amber colour from the tannin leached into it from the native scrub growing on its banks. The colloquially named sea breeze, the Fremantle Doctor, would come in about two o'clock in the afternoon, spreading welcome relief of the day's heat to the inhabitants along the coastline and inland from Perth.

Giovanni sat at a table in the dining room with his completed Entry into Australia documents. He had help from an English speaking Italian interpreter. He signed next to the date on the form where November 23, 1950 had been written for him. After the required physical examination with the ship's doctor, he'd been given a healthy tick of approval. Fortunately, he hadn't come into contact with any infectious diseases while onboard. The hand-written label on his small suitcase bore his name, and one was tied to his trunk ready for unloading when they docked at Fremantle harbour.

All he had to do now was join the queue to change his Italian lire into Australian currency of pounds, shillings and pence. It didn't look much when he was given a small handful of notes and a few coins compared to the wad of money he had handed over. He hoped he hadn't been cheated by the official bank officer who made the exchange. He had to trust it was right. In his hand he held his passport, immigration papers and a notice called the Aliens Act written in English that he couldn't read. During the journey he'd learned to say hello, yes and no and good morning and good afternoon – that was the level of progress from his English lessons. The interpreter gave them instructions to explain the procedure of how to disembark the next day.

The tugboats pulled the ship toward the pier, activity buzzed on the wharf as the heavy ropes were thrown over and tied to the bollards securing the *'Napoli'* in place. Gangplanks were lowered, and the crew began to shepherd the people who were to disembark at Fremantle into a neat line for an orderly exit. Other passengers who would continue the journey to Melbourne in the eastern states, watched from the railings above. A sign stretched across the terminal building, WELCOME TO WESTERN AUSTRALIA. Giovanni was unaware of what the words were, but the anticipation of a new beginning was coursing through his veins. Stepping onto the gangplank, he let out a slow breath, he was in Australia. The sun was rising in the vast blue sky. The glare from reflected light off the water forced him to put his hand over his eyes to see where he was going.

Giovanni chatted to the Italians he'd befriended on the voyage as he patiently waited in the long queue. The Immigration Department checked the passengers' documents against their list for each person. It was a slow process, tiring and especially frustrating when a problem arose that had to be sorted out. Some of the women and children were upset and broke down and cried. There were only two interpreters, which slowed the progress even more, none of the passengers could speak English.

As he walked out of the hot terminal building into bright sunshine, the taste of a fresh salty breeze felt good on his face. He looked around and noticed the activity at Fremantle Harbour's Victoria Quay. There was a fishing vessel where seagulls hovered overhead, hoping for an easy feed. Cranes unloaded shipping containers onto the dock, wharfies yelled out instructions and waved hand signals to the operators. A group of people behind a fence waited to meet passengers. Some held up signs with names written on them, and there was one he recognised. It was his name, and Giovanni smiled, relieved his sponsor was there to collect him as pre-arranged. He introduced himself, and vigorously shook Peter Caraffa's hand in grateful greeting. Peter suggested they walk to The Esplanade Hotel and buy some lunch while they waited for his luggage to be delivered to the baggage hall.

Giovanni listened to the different languages being spoken amongst those on the pier, some of which he understood because he heard the loud voices of some Italian dock workers or deckhands working on local fishing boats. Peter had emigrated from Sondrio in Lombardy, and he spoke the same dialect, so communication wasn't a problem. After lunch, and still a bit unsteady on his sea legs, Giovanni returned to the hall to collect his trunk, which together with Peter, they hefted onto the tray of the Model T Ford utility.

The long drive to Albany commenced from Fremantle to the Perth hills where Albany Highway went through Armadale. Never before had Giovanni seen such long distances between settlements, as they called them in Australia, not villages like they did back home. They stopped several times to get fuel for the vehicle and drink some water and then continued to journey along the bitumen road for hundreds of miles. They approached the outskirts of Albany by early evening, it was quite dark, and he could only see the lights in a few windows as they drove past town to Peter's place. Giovanni was stiff and sore after such a long day. The only other vehicle he'd ever been in was an army truck during the war. He'd usually travelled by train, on a mule or on snow skis, or else by boat or a bicycle in Italy.

Peter and Teresa gave Giovanni a meal, showed him to his room where he would be boarding and explained he would commence work in the morning after breakfast. Tired and ready for bed, Giovanni decided to have a wash and quickly unpack some of his clothes for the next day. The open trunk revealed an envelope addressed to him sitting on top of the pile of neatly folded shirts and trousers. He picked it up and caressed Emilia's handwriting. A sudden emotion welled up inside him, and tears trickled down the side of his face. He thought, 'Oh, God, I hope I've done the right thing'.

October 29, 1950

Dear Giovanni

Even though I know you will open this after our wedding anniversary, I wanted to date it the 29th of October, so you knew I was thinking about us and our marriage while we are separated by the vast sea you have just crossed. When you're gone, it will feel strange knowing you aren't just a train ride or two to get home anymore. My heart already feels heavy with the loss of your presence, but I know your love and thoughts will be with me every day. You are my rock. A part of me cannot live without knowing you're doing this for your family. I take comfort in understanding the importance of your choice and support your decision.

It was difficult to accept at first, but your determination to make it work encourages me. You must have the sun shining on you in Australia, not cold and miserable like it is here. They say the sun always shines there, is that true? Tell me about your journey and of the new things you see and learn every day.

All our love and prayers are with you, and we're longing to hear from you, so please write to us as soon as you can.

Your wife, Emilia

Giovanni sat and stared at the short note, encouraged he should press on and do what he'd come to achieve, a better life for them all. If he could make a lot of money soon, he'd return to Italy, but that was unlikely. However, if the family came here, and their finances improved, they could go back home if they didn't want to stay. After all, he only had a temporary visa that expired in two years, and he was expected to complete that commitment.

A new life pattern had begun to emerge at the Caraffa's place. Their property on Robinson Road was about a ten-minute car ride from town. Breakfast was a bowl of cooked rolled oats with some milk, porridge they called it, tasteless but filling for a hungry worker. Giovanni had been set to work straight away, the day after he arrived. Peter had shown him where to find the tools and bags of cement in the shed at the back of the block. He'd mix a batch of concrete and place half a shovel of it in block moulds, give them a shake then put an empty brown beer bottle in the middle and top it up with more concrete. After it set, no-one would know a bottle was inside. Interesting concept thought Giovanni.

He worked all day under the shade of gum trees, and annoying bush flies got in his eyes. The sounds of unfamiliar birds often caught his attention. In the middle of the day, he ate the hastily made salami sandwich Teresa had given him with a flask of water. Dinner was a pasta dish with a bit of beef, some fruit and finally, a cup of espresso coffee. It was another Saturday morning, and it started the same as any other day, but today he was going to build a retaining wall with the concrete blocks from the stockpile. They'd loaded the trailer with some of the blocks and equipment, and Peter dropped him off in town to work on the project.

It was a mild day, quiet and one for contemplation. Thoughts whirled around in Giovanni's head. He wanted answers for some of his questions, so he would have to talk to Peter. After work when the utility pulled up, Giovanni got in and began to fire away with his arsenal of questions.

"How much will I earn? Can I open a bank account? Is there some land I can buy at a price I can afford? Where is it? How much does it cost? What will I have to do to start building a house? How are houses built in Australia? They look different to buildings in Italy, where should I start?"

Peter smiled at his enthusiastic companion.

"Slow down mate, one thing at a time. First of all, you gotta pay back the money you owe for the fare out here, and then there's the cost of the trip from Perth to Albany. Your board has to come out of what you earn as well. It's gonna take time, mate." Peter continued. "The first couple of months is gonna be covering your bills, you might get a bit left over, but you'll have to work seven days a week if you wanna do more. Okay mate? We can go to the bank at lunchtime one day next week and get a savings account sorted for you if you like. And as for some land and building, maybe put those ideas on hold for now, eh?"

Feeling a bit disillusioned but understanding all these things were necessary, Giovanni nodded and stared out the window. He was silent the rest of the way back to the house.

Digging in the trunk to find a pen and paper, Giovanni moved a coat aside and as he did he discovered something wrapped in a towel. It was their framed photo. Emotion surged through him. He placed the frame on the small table next to the bed where he could see it every day and remind himself all this would be worth it. He decided to write about the good things he'd experienced so far. How he'd seen the strange looking kangaroos hop around in the bush and listened to magpies sing in the early morning and cockatoos squawk at sunset.

He couldn't explain the scents on the air, the aroma of the grey-green eucalyptus trees and brown Boronia or the smell of the damp soil after a shower of rain. He could describe the unique plants he'd seen and told of wattle trees that bloom with bright yellow balls of fluff and how the arum lily, originally from South Africa, grew everywhere in the swampy areas around here. The flower was pure white, looked as smooth as velvet and had a long yellow stamen in the centre of the single wrap-around-petal, the flower stood out against the lush green leaves. The summer was mild, and they had showers of rain on some days, but the sky was a pale blue with scattered fluffy white clouds skidding along on the breeze.

Giovanni couldn't say anything about his lonely existence, about missing his family in a way he could never have imagined possible or, as impressive as this country was, how he longed to breathe mountain air and see bright green leaves fluttering on the trees. He didn't mention being covered in mosquito bites that itched and bled from scratching them or how exhausted he was from working every day from sun up at 5.00am to sundown at 7.30pm.

He lifted his eyes from the page and looked at the photo of Emilia and himself, and the one of the children. He recalled every curve of their faces, the depth in their eyes, the feel of their skin and hair against his cheek when he kissed them. Giovanni reached across and gently passed a finger over each one of them. Love and the need to provide for his family filled every fibre of his being, he could do this, and he would do it for them.

On an early January afternoon in Italy, it was cold, and the light was fading. Emilia quickened her step as she headed for home wanting to get back as soon as she could. Her mother-in-law was taking care of the children while she visited her parents for an uninterrupted conversation about a combined birthday celebration for Rosanna, Cesare and herself. Her heart was heavy as she pulled the knitted scarf closer around her neck and tucked it into her wool jacket.

She couldn't help feeling resentful lately of how hard the last few months had been. What was my husband thinking, she thought, to come home one day and tell me he'd decided it was time to start a new life, in a new place, and then off he went. Close to tears, she remembered his face, ruggedly handsome with those large deep soulful eyes, oh how she missed him. It was different from when he was away during the war, even with all the risks she knew he would come home if he could.

Emilia smiled weakly, wiping the dampness at the corner of her eyes that threatened to spill over onto her cheeks. She remembered those short breaks during the war years when they would walk hand-in-hand along the path by the river. They enjoyed the sunshine on their faces and treasured every moment of being in each other's company, and then, of course, there were the children who came along after those encounters. There was no point letting her mind wander down that train of thought, it was all a bit depressing, thinking of what had been.

Post-war troubles abounded. There was no work and only a little food available, and what Emilia could buy had to be run up on the tab at Formigalli's store. The kind old man was happy to let her do that considering her circumstances. Hopefully, he wouldn't have to wait too long before Giovanni could send money through to cover the costs. The children needed nourishment and Mama, Papa and Silvia and Cesare only had just so much they could share. What a blessing they were, Emilia couldn't even begin to imagine what she would've done without them. They were stoic, reassuring, loving and kindness itself.

She walked in through the door, and the warmth of their home enveloped her. At least she was safe and comfortable here, so were the children. Rosanna was nearly seven, Cesare would be six soon, and Silvana turned four last November. She'd cried herself to sleep wanting her daddy after her birthday party. Emilia thought it was a good thing that at least she still remembered him. Hopefully, they wouldn't forget about their father who was missing every part of their young lives. Rosanna had started school and Cesare wasn't far from joining her. Silvana wanted to go too but she wasn't old enough yet, she cried every morning when they left Rosanna at the gate.

Progress on the building site in Grey Street East near the Albany post office continued. Several tradesmen including carpenters, plumbers and electricians worked alongside Giovanni as he lay more blocks in the wall. A local passed by, calling out unkind words.

"Go home, you wog!"

Giovanni smiled and responded.

"*Si*, yes, I make *casa*, home for my *famiglia*, they come here too."

The man spat on the ground.

"You greasy ding. Go back to where you came from, we don't want you here."

Geoff walked up beside Giovanni and nudged him with his elbow.

"Don't listen to him mate, he isn't worth taking seriously."

Confused, Giovanni was sure he'd understood but apparently because of his poor language skills he'd missed something in the conversation. He appreciated Geoff Preston's friendship. He liked the tall, lanky English electrician with thick glasses and big teeth who called himself 'a £10 pom' and had a great sense of humour. Geoff helped Giovanni out whenever possible. He understood the plight of being an immigrant, even though he didn't share the language or cultural barriers Giovanni faced.

The dawn of the first Saturday in July crept in, the day set aside to make sausage and salami every year. Peter and Giovanni had finished work early one day during the week to slaughter the fattened pig and had butchered it ready for the weekend. Several family members joined in the process of mincing the pork, adding herbs and spices and mixing it before bagging it into the cleaned gut used as sausage skins. They made links of sausages and salami for drying.

It felt a bit like home to Giovanni, the smells, the chatter and the polenta and sausage meal they ate for lunch was all comfortably familiar. After cleaning up, the salami was hung in the cellar by their strings and out came a piano accordion and the home-made claret while they sang the songs from Italy with gusto. All the work and social interaction made it a most enjoyable day, Giovanni's best day yet in Australia. Peter had arranged for him to purchase a seven-acre lot at the back of his property, and in just a few weeks time, he would start building his house on Elphinstone Road. It was exciting and a relief to finally be making headway with his plans.

"Rosanna, come here right now and help me with this." Emilia snapped at her eldest daughter who turned and faced her mother with a confused and frightened look on her face. Emilia was immediately remorseful.

"I'm sorry, sweetheart. Mama's just tired and not coping very well today. I didn't mean to be nasty to you, please come and hold the door for me while I take this basket of washing outside." Rosanna did as she was asked and then willingly helped her mother by passing her clothes and pegs ready to put them on the washing line. Emilia couldn't understand why she felt like she did.

"After we've done the chores, we're going to get ready for a train ride to Sondrio and visit Carla and the twins. It'll cheer us up. Well, it will cheer me up anyway. If they're not home, we'll go and get a gelato and make it a special day."

August 19, 1951

Dear Giovanni,

Anna-Maria has gone. She left to sail to Argentina last week. There'd been some underhanded goings-on in Antonio's family. Someone had written to him saying Anna-Maria was flirting with other men, which was entirely untrue.

She had wondered why he hadn't written for such a long time. Of course, she thought he was too busy preparing for her to come, or that maybe he had found someone else. Anyway, when she found out, she wrote to Antonio straight away and told him she was coming. They were married by proxy, and there was no further delay. She is so brave, much more than I am, Anna-Maria has never even left Morbegno. At least I've been to Milano, Somma Lombardo and Bardonecchia. It was difficult to say goodbye; we will be a fractured family, dispersed across the world. Nino took her to the port at Genoa and saw her off. He'd applied to emigrate too but was sick on the day of his appointment for a medical examination, and he decided not to go to the doctor or to go overseas.

Mama and Papa are unhappy, Anna-Maria is only 19, and they don't ever expect to see her again or meet their grandchildren one day. I know my leaving in the future is weighing heavily on them as well. At least they have the exciting news of Nino and Adriana's baby due in February. Adriana is keeping quite well.

Carla sends her greetings. I took the children on the train yesterday to visit her in Sondrio. The twins have grown up and are a handsome pair, Raph would've been proud of them. It's sad he never knew them. Gina and Antonio have a touching emotional connection to Nunzio now they see him every day. That man has such patience with them. They are much like their mother in nature with so much energy, unlike Raphael's quiet disposition.

I noticed Nunzio and Carla looking at each other with affection too. They would be a good match, and I was surprised Carla didn't gush on about their relationship. She has matured and changed with the circumstances life has given her. I suppose that's a good thing, her sparkle is still there though.

I wasn't going to tell you how I've been feeling lately, but I know if I don't I will carry this burden around and continue to be melancholy. Yesterday I was miserable. I snapped at Rosanna, and she wasn't doing anything wrong. Poor little girl, she is such a gem and always so helpful and senses my needs, much like you do, but she is a child, and I can't explain to her how difficult this separation from you feels.

I haven't been feeling well, it takes all my energy to get out of bed in the morning, and I want to hide away from everyone and everything.

I have to put on a face that people expect to see. It would be cruel to the children and our parents if I fell apart but I feel like I am on the brink of doing just that, it's too hard living without you Giovanni.

How I long to be beside you in our bed, to wash your clothes and prepare your meals, to be able to share my thoughts and feelings with you every day. I need to know you're safe and well, I worry so much it's making me sick. I want to be the wife to you I promised to be and the mother to our children that they deserve. I know the small incident I described doesn't sound that bad but there is much more behind it, and it frightens me. I'm only just holding it together. Please help me to know what I should do, I need you, and I love you.

Write to me soon, I long for and wait every day for a letter from you. The children send their love and miss you too. We pray for you every day.

Your wife, Emilia

Giovanni took another nail from his carpenter's leather bag, picked up the hammer and rammed it straight into the jarrah timber frame. Memories of his home where towering snow-capped mountains stood covered in pine and birch trees with the Adda River winding its way through the Valtellina in Italy flooded his thoughts. How different it was to the eucalyptus and Australian weeping willow growing nearby on the block of land he had purchased. He'd worked incredibly hard to pay for it.

The months were flying by, one day bleeding into the next. His spare time was spent building the house on his property about five miles from town. He had paid back his borrowed money to sail from Genoa to Fremantle and some of the other outstanding debts he owed. Now he had the determination to save all he could to prepare for his family to come and join him. It was a struggle, not being able to speak the language very well; the food was different, the sights, the sounds, in fact, pretty much everything was different.

Everyone called him Jack here, probably because they didn't know how to pronounce Giovanni. Jack knew it was worth the difficulties he faced and had to get through each day even though the loneliness was almost unbearable. He nearly hit his thumb with the hammer because he wasn't paying attention to what he was doing.

When he finally fell into bed at night, he would think of his Emilia, her fine features, soft skin, and oh-so-soft hair. He would think of his little ones and wonder how much they had grown and whether they even remembered who he was anymore. Jack often considered if this was the right thing to do, but he knew it was. The pain of separation still bore a hole in his heart that burned with a sense of loss he couldn't explain. How intrinsically woven were their hearts, even with the distance that separated them. Emilia was his lover, soul mate and friend; their son and daughters were his life.

He hoped they were all right. He would try and write another letter this week if he could keep his eyes open long enough to do it. It took a long time to communicate with each other; thankfully the Suez Canal was clear of the debris of war to make the passage for ships shorter now. Mail would get through quicker, and it would be a better journey for his family.

When the house was built, he could start saving money for their fares so they could come to join him. He owed money in Italy for his family's needs and had to pay that back as well. Jack wondered how much longer it would take to get on top of all this, utterly exhausted, his mind began to slip into a fog, and he fell asleep.

Even though he boarded with Peter and Teresa, he didn't see very much of them. After work he would have dinner, then go down the road to his place and work by lamplight because the days were shorter during winter. At breakfast time, Teresa had put an envelope on the table where Jack sat. It was strange it was given to him in the morning since the mail was delivered during the day and it wasn't there last night. A letter from home, he wanted to open it, but he had to go to work. He wouldn't read it in front of them, so he put it on his pillow for when he got home later.

All day thoughts of the letter plagued him. He had an idea something wasn't quite right. As soon as they pulled up, Jack went straight inside and ripped open the envelope to read Emilia's letter. He ran his hand over his head and pushed his fingers through his hair; it wasn't good news and Emilia's state of mind concerned him greatly. The sick feeling he had in his stomach grew, and he determined his family would have to come sooner rather than later.

The photos on the little table had lost their ability for him to sense their nearness for some time. It was hard to recall their touch, their scent and expressions or to remember their voices anymore. Springtime wasn't far away, and if he pushed himself harder with the longer days, maybe they could come by Christmas. He hoped Emilia would be able to hang in there with the knowledge that in a few more months they could be reunited. Replying to her in haste, he encouraged her to prevail and told her the ticket would be on its way soon.

CHAPTER FIFTEEN

The Time Has Come

FORMIGALLI'S DELICATESSEN, IN THE CENTRE of Morbegno, stocked cheeses and grocery items. The shelves provided shoppers with more variety lately. Emilia went to the counter with her small basket of essentials and asked for the things to be added to her list. Signora Formigalli hauled out the massive ledger and opened it to the Nostrini page, surprise lit her face.

"Well, look at that, we received a payment from Giovanni this week, and your balance is right down. You must be so proud of your husband. He's doing well over there in Australia, Emilia."

She nodded to acknowledge the compliment but ducked her head down and pretended to fuss with her purchases as she blinked away tears. It was a good sign, though, wasn't it?

Emilia trudged up the stairs to the excited sounds of the children laughing out loud. A shriek from Silvana sounded while her Nonna hopped around like a kangaroo to catch her. Silvia was taking care of them, they were playing together and making up stories. They hadn't heard her come into the kitchen and start to put the food away.

"We promise not to tell Mama you told us about your letter from Papa. She gets sad and cries when she gets his letters. We go off and play quietly, and when she feels better we know we can be noisy again," Rosanna said.

Quite shocked at the statement, Emilia hadn't realised her response to Giovanni's letters affected the children. An envelope with an

Australian stamp in the corner was sitting on the bench near the bread crock. Silvia must have put it there after the postman had come while she was away. She sighed, both longing and dreading to find out what he had to say. It would be better to wait until bedtime to open it, and then she could cry without upsetting her family.

When Emilia picked up the mail she realised there were two envelopes, one from Giovanni and another one from Genoa. Giovanni's letter had been posted over a month ago. A sudden realisation began to dawn on her, with shaking hands she opened the Italian letter postmarked three days earlier. Inside was one adult and three children's Tourist Class tickets for the *'Oceania'* sailing from Genoa in February. A letter and light blue brochure from the Lloyd Triestino Lines accompanied the tickets explaining the process, how much luggage was allowed and a passport for Emilia, with the children to travel under her name, would be needed.

They would be advised when they were to leave from Genoa and would call into the ports at Naples, Messina, Port Said, Suez, Colombo, Djakarta and then Fremantle where they would disembark. Australian immigration papers and visas would be provided and processed from the Consulate in Milano. Smallpox vaccinations were required to enter Australia.

Nervous anticipation consumed her because she had to do this by herself and had no idea how to go about it. In the quiet of her room, Emilia took Giovanni's letter and opened it. He was beside himself with pleasure that they would be coming to join him at last. He explained how, unfortunately, the house wouldn't be finished, but they would manage. It was more important to be together than concern themselves with a few minor issues that could be solved as they went along. Giovanni told Emilia to ask Nino to help her sort out the paperwork. She hadn't thought of that and was relieved at the suggestion. Giovanni had also written to his brother-in-law with details of what needed to be done before his family left Italy. Now it was time to prepare for the journey that would bring them together again.

The family gathered to share their last Christmas in Morbegno. They attended midnight mass, had mulled wine and amoretti biscuits on Christmas Eve as they had done for as long as Emilia could remember. The children had been excited and enjoyed the celebration and then fallen into exhausted sleep not long after they'd returned home. As she sat in the warmth of their second storey flat, Emilia began to feel an anxious knot grow in the pit of her stomach. The realisation hit her that she was to leave everything she had ever known behind. Tears flowed, and she sobbed into her pillow.

After their tenth wedding anniversary, alone, seven weeks ago, she longed to join Giovanni in Australia. The cost of leaving their parents and family behind seemed unbearable but what could she do? She couldn't have both and being with her husband was her heart's greatest desire. Emilia was unaware her mother and mother-in-law were in emotional turmoil at the same time as they contemplated the coming departure of their loved daughter and grandchildren.

A clear day dawned in southern Western Australia on Christmas Day in 1951. Jack could barely remember last Christmas because it wasn't long after he first arrived in this new land. He'd been challenged by all the changes in his life at the time. It felt strange not to have a snowy winter's day to celebrate the Christmas season.

Peter and Teresa were going to take him to Mass with them at 8.30am in town at St Joseph's Catholic Church in Aberdeen Street. The building was small and uncomplicated compared to the Chiesa San Giovanni Battista in Morbegno which was quite austere from the outside but huge and well adorned inside. He didn't get to church much anymore because he worked on his house as often as he could. Memories of a long-ago service on the Christmas Eve he'd asked Emilia if he could court her, then the day they were married, and the children's baptisms swamped his mind. Thoughts of when he might again darken the Italian village church's doorstep enveloped him, for all he knew, he may never return.

A summer Christmas gave him more time to spend at the house during the holiday period. It would be two months before the family would arrive and the more work he got finished before then, the better for Emilia's sake. The roof timbers were up, and he had ordered the tin sheeting, so while he waited for it, Jack continued to line the top section of the walls above the block work. The bathroom still needed lining, and an outside laundry and toilet were next on his list of 'to do' items. A slow smile spread across his face, not long to go now and his family would be where they belonged, with him.

Rosanna turned nine on her shared birthday with her Mama, their last one with family in their home village on the Adda River. On January 29, Cesarino had a birthday cake at morning tea time with eight candles on it. One big puff and he blew them all out at once, his smile almost split his face he was so proud of himself. They made it a special day with Carla, Nunzio and the twins. It was a tearful and difficult day for them all, their last visit and a final goodbye. In two days they would leave to go to Genoa, ready to board the *'Oceania'*.

One trunk was packed with all the possessions they were to take, wrapped in towels, sheets and clothing. Another one held all their clothes and the few special toys, books and treasures that belonged to the children. A large suitcase for Emilia and a small one each for the children were packed with the clothes and toiletries for the journey across the sea. The documents they needed and Emilia's passport sat on the table in the middle of the room. She looked around her barren home and contemplated the memories, some happy and others that were more difficult to bring to mind. She was leaving. A hollow numbness settled over her, and she pushed aside the raw emotion that roiled through her. Nino knocked on the door and let himself in.

"Ready, Emilia?" it was more of a statement than a question.

"I don't know Nino. I'm not sure about anything except that this is really happening."

He was accompanying his sister to the port to help with the luggage, the children and give her moral support. They would all stay at Mimi's parents' house in Genoa to rest for one night before they boarded the ship. Standing perfectly still beside the warmth in the hearth, Emilia nodded at her brother with a blank look on her face. She knew Silvia and Cesare were downstairs making the most of their last opportunity with the children. While Nino loaded their luggage, Emilia embraced her parents-in-law and her resolve left her. Tears soaked Cesare's shoulder, and Silvia sobbed alongside them, it all felt unbearable, and then the children began to cry.

"We have to be strong and help each other," Emilia remarked quietly. The adults pulled their emotions together long enough to wave goodbye as they headed down the street toward Rosa and Lorenzo's.

"You'll get through this Emilia," Nino whispered. His strength propped her up as they faced the rest of the family. Handkerchiefs were soaked through, eyes red and swollen, mouths dry as parting words left their lips. Emilia and her mother hugged each other fiercely, neither wanted to let the other go. Franca embraced her sister one last time, and Papa stood aside with a vacant stare, unable to say anything more with the enormous lump of emotion choking his vocal chords. The sad troupe bundled up and went to the railway station to wait on the platform for the regional train to come along the tracks and take them to their first destination.

"All aboard," Cesare called out in a strained voice to the passengers as the final minutes ticked by, he waved his flag, and the train lurched away from the station. The children leaned out of the window and waved to their Nonno until they couldn't see him. Three gloomy children sat on the firm bench seat opposite their mother and uncle. No-one said a word or looked at anyone else. They stared out of the window or found a mental space to escape to and avoided eye contact.

Their eggshell-like emotions would have cracked and spilt out if any one of them dared to make a sound.

By the time they reached the view of Lago di Como, Nino had pointed out the different villages to the children and explained how they would go into more tunnels through the mountains soon. As they approached Milano Centrale, the excitement of seeing other trains and tracks and the station helped to ease their discomfort. A train change was necessary, their entire luggage had to be dragged off, and they needed to wait for the connecting train to arrive. The children went for a walk around the terminal, fascinated with all they saw.

Zio Peppino and Zia Chiara came running toward them, glad they'd caught them before they left. A jumbled conversation with hugs and kisses and tears and good wishes and promises to write were made as Nino and Peppino loaded the luggage into the carriage of their next train. Two hours later, they arrived in Genoa. After they stowed the luggage away for collection in the morning, Nino introduced his sister and her family to Mimi's parents. Their kind welcome put them at ease as they shared a meal together. Emilia excused herself to arrange baths for the children and put them to bed early after a long emotional day. A bit of quiet space in the bathroom felt good before she went to bed herself. Nervous anticipation of the events to come kept her from sleep for most of the night.

Emilia braced herself at dawn, said a prayer for help and safety, and got herself and her family ready to leave. A throng of passengers along the dock at Genoa harbour crowded around them. Dotted among the people were clusters of families who cried and clung to each other. Parents wailed as they released their young adult daughters who were to travel alone. Emilia faced the sleek white ship with its yellow funnel and blue and white shipping company emblem, an anchor and a crown with the initials LT on its bow. She held Silvana's hand and walked up the gangway. Cesare and Rosanna were excited to be going on a great adventure. Emilia was thankful they'd said their goodbyes in private before leaving home, it was hard enough to farewell her brother. It was an exciting day for him though because he'd received a telegram early this morning to say Adriana had gone into labour. Nino was anxious to get back home, so he quickly arranged all the necessary transfers of luggage into the hold and made sure the paperwork was done. He bent down to hug his nephew and nieces, gave them a sweet to cheer them and then turned to his beloved sister. A deep sense of belonging enveloped them. Nothing could ever take that away. They embraced, kissed each other's cheeks, and Nino walked away.

Emilia's tears slipped silently down her face, glad he wasn't going to wave goodbye. He needed to get back home, and she didn't think she could bear to see him stand there as they left their homeland. Nino wiped his eyes as he rounded the corner of the building where he had stopped to turn around and take one last look as they all disappeared into the lobby doorway. Now he had to get back to Adriana, hopefully before nightfall.

CHAPTER SIXTEEN

Oceania

STAFF IN THE LOBBY GAVE directions for the family to find their allotted accommodation on C Deck. The metal stairs led down into the bowels of the ship where they found their four bunks among many others. Emilia tucked away cases, pulled the curtains across the bunks and looked for the bathroom, and then they decided to go up on deck to watch the scene below. She noticed other young women like herself travelling with children. There was a mother, with two daughters at the top of the gangway, who spoke loudly in Italian with a strong German accent. Emilia wondered at her preference of travelling with an Italian shipping company but supposed there probably weren't many other options available.

Tourist-class women and children were directed one way, and men were sent to where the male dormitory was located at the opposite end of the vessel. First-class passengers were ushered to their cabins by a crew member carrying luggage, while second-class cabin occupants were issued with a key and a deck map.

Once everyone was on board, a loud horn sounded to signal their departure. Streamers were thrown from the Promenade deck down to the dock. It created a carnival atmosphere that Emilia thought no-one was in the mood for but because of tradition, it was done anyway. Some passengers felt it kept them connected to their loved ones for a bit longer, but she thought it would just prolong the agony. Tugboats pulled the large vessel through the harbour, avoiding small craft, ferries and cargo ships. Weak late morning sunshine highlighted the elegant pastel buildings where green trees of parklands stood out against the shadowy mountains behind. The Ligurian coast faded into a blurred line on the horizon as they sailed away.

Early evening light came as they headed across the Tyrrhenian Sea while dinner was served in the second-class dining room. They ate soup served in a cup, a salad with some fish and finished with peaches and ice-cream. Rosanna, Cesare and Silvana loved the novelty of a ship dinner. They all felt a bit queasy from the movement on the sea. Emilia bathed the children and put them in their bunks, excited chatter kept them awake for a time, but they were soon sound asleep. Her night was spent visiting the toilet.

In the morning she still felt quite ill but forced herself to go to breakfast and tried to eat a piece of dry toast. That didn't stay down either. Tired and sore from vomiting, Emilia put herself to bed after she took the children to the play room. Rosanna was in charge of her brother and sister while their Mama was sick. The children had recovered from their seasickness quickly. Emilia spent most of her time in a weak state upon her bed. Other women helped to take care of her and looked out for the three siblings who were well behaved and polite.

When the ship docked at Napoli, Emilia managed to struggle up on deck for some fresh air and a little sunshine. A kerfuffle on the gangplank caught their attention. Everyone stopped and stared at a young man and a more mature woman in a struggle. She thrashed about trying to go back to the pier while he endeavoured to steer her forward.

"Dom, I will not go. You can't make me," she yelled. Embarrassed by the episode, he calmly encouraged his aunt to board the ship.

"Come on Zia Maria, you are going to Zio Manuele in Australia. He is waiting for you." A man picked up the case she had nearly dropped into the sea below while her nephew held her by the hand and forcefully dragged her along to the lobby. He sighed and thanked the man who helped with the luggage.

"Grazie, Signore, mille grazie."

The woman cried as she rocked back and forth on a chair muttering in dialect. Domenico found out their cabin locations and arranged an escort for his aunt to her berth. At four o'clock in the afternoon, the ship headed off to the Messina Strait between the boot of mainland Italy and the island of Sicily.

Soon the large golden statue of the Madonnina guarding the entrance to the harbour at Messina was visible. More passengers embarked here for their journey to Australia and eight children joined the others in the play room that day. The aft deck was crammed with people who wanted to embed the memory of their country in their mind as they left it behind. Light and shadows played on the rugged formation of the steep hills of southern Italy. White cottages dotted the landscape, and an old fortress tower stood a perpetual silent sentinel. Soon the province of Reggio Calabria and the island of Sicily disappeared into the sea as the *'Oceania'* surged ahead on the waves of the Mediterranean.

The ship had taken anchor in Port Said for nearly a week, and the lull in movement made everyone restless. It was usual for ships to have to wait a few days to allow other vessels to come through the Suez Canal before they could enter it. But no-one understood why they were not going anywhere for so long.

The eerie quietness encouraged rumours to abound. Some passengers said pirates lurked along the waterway, or a boat had been sunk in the canal, and others said they were to return to Italy. The Captain called a meeting, and all passengers had to report to their lounges. Emilia sat in a chair by an open window with her children gathered at her feet on the floor. The second-class lounge was crowded with people crammed in on the seats, and others stood in any available space.

An announcement was made that the halt in the ship's progress was due to a safety issue. Two weeks earlier a significant conflict in Ismailia between the Egyptian police and the British Army who patrolled the Suez zone had given cause for concern. After demands to hand over weapons and resistance from the Egyptians, shooting broke out until the police had run out of ammunition and surrendered to the British. Men had been killed and wounded. The following weekend, riots and arson attacks in Cairo caused significant damage to European owned buildings and businesses.

Consideration had been given by the company to sail around Africa instead. However, they decided to sit tight and wait for further reports. The management wanted to be sure it was safe to proceed especially considering they were a Trieste based shipping company headed toward a Commonwealth country. Order in the area was restored, and now they waited for the banked up shipping lane to clear.

Fortunately, Rosanna, Cesare and Silvana adapted to ship life easily. They enjoyed the activities in the play room, loved exploring the nooks and crannies of the ship and helped staff in the second-class dining room to clear tables after they ate their meal, ready for the next sitting. Early one evening as they took up plates to put on the trolley, there was a loud scream from the Lido deck. People rushed to see what had happened. More cries were heard.

"Help, someone, please help me!" Domenico shouted.

Maria had climbed up and attempted to jump overboard, but her foot was tangled in a rope looped between a lifeboat and the railing. She was dangling upside down over the side of the ship. The young man who'd picked up the suitcase on the gangplank was on hand again.

"You've got your hands full with this one, haven't you? My name's Antonino. It looks like we're to be friends if I have to keep coming to rescue you and your aunt."

A sailor saw them and was about to call, 'Man overboard', but the young men had managed to haul Maria back to safety on the deck. She sobbed violently and shook all over.

"I want to go home. I can get a boat back from here. Let me go, let me...go, please. Let me..." her voice faltered, and she began to hiccup.

The sailor gave them a blanket and advised them to take her to the ship's doctor downstairs. The doctor sedated Maria and kept her under observation for the night. After an in-depth consultation, he gave a prescribed medication to calm her down while they were aboard ship until they arrived in Fremantle. He wrote a medical note in English for her to take to a general practitioner after she disembarked in Australia. Maria was stable for the rest of the journey. She sat quietly in the lounge and stared out the window, not noticing any activity around her at all. Domenico was always by her side, and Antonino would play cards or chat with him. Often Giovanni and Bruno who had boarded the *'Oceania'* in Genoa joined them.

The 163 kilometre man-made Suez Canal was built straight and deep from Port Said to the Gulf of Suez. The canal was interesting to the children initially, and sometimes they would see fishermen in tiny boats throwing out their nets, an occasional village, or a military camp along the way.

It didn't take long before they became bored with the same view of the endless golden desert sand on both sides of the canal. Curiosity took precedence over the fear there might be risks of danger with the current political issues as they passed by Ismailia. All they could see were tall date palms lining the quiet roads. Several women carried six or seven woven baskets on their heads and old men sat outside the doors of their houses, smoked a pipe and watched the ship go by. It all seemed quite subdued.

Cargo ships loaded with sea containers were moored in the Great Bitter Lake waiting for access to go through the next section of the canal. The *'Oceania'* sailed into the port at Suez where they restocked with fuel, fresh food and water. They headed toward the Gulf of Aden through the Red Sea with Egypt and Sudan on the right bank and Saudi Arabia on the left.

In Colombo, on the island of Ceylon adventurous passengers alighted to meet the locals, bargain for a souvenir and see the sights. The tantalising aroma of delicious curry available from stalls along the pier wafted on the gentle breeze. Exotic purchases were wrapped carefully and stowed away by those who could afford such a privilege.

Emilia became sick again when they were out in the Indian Ocean, unable to do anything for the children, and barely capable of looking after herself. Rosanna would bring a bowl of clear soup and a piece of toast when her mother felt she could take some nourishment.

A cluster of children lurked in a dark corner at the closest point to the bridge while they waited for the captain to emerge. Nine-year-old Gisella peeked around the corner to keep watch. She and her sister, Bielgard, could speak some Italian and when they weren't sure of the right words they used brusque body language to explain what they meant. None of these children paid any heed to the fact the girls were German, they were just their friends. Some mothers wouldn't allow their sons or daughters to speak to them, but others believed they all deserved a chance at a new life. They were probably no more Nazi than they were Fascist if the truth be told.

"Shh, or he'll hear us," she ordered. "We've got to be quiet."

The door to the bridge opened at exactly the right time for the captain to go and perform his regular duty in the first-class lounge. As he was about to pass by, the children pounced in front of him with huge smiles on their faces.

"Surprise," they all yelled. He welcomed their little game and watched with amusement while they giggled behind their hands.

"Mama mia, you frightened me. Maybe I don't have any sweets in my pocket today." The captain teased them while he put his hand in to pull out some wrapped sweets and gave them one each. Some days they would follow him until he turned around and saw them, other days they would run up and hug him around his legs so he couldn't walk any further until they received their treat. He loved to play their game because he missed his children while he was away at sea. It touched his heart to give them a little fun and make their day special.

After receiving their treats from the captain, they ran down to the kitchen where the staff loaded fresh bread or cakes and biscuits into their aprons. The children would go and offer it to any passengers who would like some for morning tea.

Excitement permeated the atmosphere as they approached the Equator. A crew member would dress up as King Neptune with a long white beard, crown and trident to hold court on the Lido deck near the swimming pool. Volunteer *Pollywogs*, that is, those who had not crossed the equator before, could join in the planned joviality. All the passengers gathered at 11 o'clock in the morning and watched the grass-skirted pollywogs parade around the pool. They were escorted to King Neptune by previously initiated *Shellback* crew members. Many a tall story was told, revolting tricks played and a great deal of laughter at the expense of the pollywogs was enjoyed.

At midday they were all thrown in the pool, girls screamed, and the water splashed over onto spectators like an enormous tidal wave. The swimming pool was alive with motion, people bobbing around, bottoms up with duck dives and feet exposed from underwater handstands. A deliciously grilled luncheon on the deck was the pinnacle of the occasion and certificates were given out to the brave new shellbacks. Dom, Antonini, Giovanni, and Bruno showed theirs to Zia Maria.

> Certificate of the Domain of Neptunus Rex in Latitude 000 and Longitude 85° E on the Good Ship Oceania to have been gathered into the fold as a trusty Shellback and initiated into the solemn mystery of the Ancient Order of the Deep.

The youngest passengers participated under the watchful eyes of their carers from the play room. After lunch, a wet Rosanna, Cesare and Silvana rushed down to visit Emilia and breathlessly described the raucous event while they changed into dry clothes.

Djakarta was hot and humid as they approached the Tandjong Priok harbour. The unpleasant odour of fermented rotten soy beans in barrels on the dock putrified the air. Most passengers decided to remain indoors because it was too uncomfortable on deck. The final leg of the voyage was about to begin, and it was a welcome relief to know it would soon be over after the week of sitting out at sea with nothing but ocean as far as the eye could see.

Emilia was desperately lonely. The children were content to entertain themselves, but she wanted them close for a change. When Rosanna came down with her soup, she asked her to sit and talk instead of running off to play. A few minutes later all three were on her bunk to tell her about the stinky place outside. They screwed up their noses and shuddered at the thought, happy they didn't have to go and live there. They huddled around Emilia to talk about their father. The eagerness in their voices about the reunion was a welcome relief from the grey world that had been Emilia's existence on the ship. Thoughts of Giovanni flooded her with warmth, not long to go now.

As the ship sailed toward Western Australia, the waters became rough. Crew members worked quickly to fold up deck chairs and umbrellas and put away all loose items. A cyclone hovered along the north-western coast of Australia near Onslow. Everyone had to make sure all windows and doors were closed tight. Strong winds and rain lashed against the vessel which caused it to pitch on the heaving sea.

Passengers were warned not to go out onto the deck. In the dining room plates and utensils had to be held onto while they were eating. Emilia suffered the worst seasickness of the entire journey in those last few days aboard. Rosanna stayed by her mother's side to empty the sick bowl because her Mama was too weak to make it to the bathroom.

Giovanni was wearing a track in the gravel driveway from pacing back and forth waiting for Peter to come and pick him up. His small overnight bag sat on a concrete block beside the front door. He was anxious to leave and kept checking his watch, with only minutes ticking by. Geoff was driving the extra vehicle they were using to transport the family and their luggage to Albany. Emilia and the children were arriving in Fremantle tomorrow at 6.00am. The men were going to travel to Perth and stay the night with some Italian friends. Finally, he could hear the utility coming up the road. Peter drove through town and then headed up the highway on their way to Perth with Geoff following behind them.

The warm running water from the shower was refreshing. Emilia was bathing and washing her hair unassisted today. After drying herself off with the towel, and putting on her underwear, she pulled her dress over her head and did up the buttons. Her dress hung loosely about her small frame because she'd lost a lot of weight over the past few weeks. Emilia noticed her pale face reflected in the mirror. She tried pinching her cheeks to give them a little bit of colour, hoping it would help her to look better.

It took all her effort dressing three excited children in their best clothes and doing their hair while they wriggled around. They looked lovely, she thought, healthy and suntanned. Exhausted, Emilia took them upstairs and sat in the lounge while she watched them play with their friends for the last time. She had to keep reminding them to be careful to keep clean. All the necessary immigration procedures had been taken care of, and now they were waiting for their final port of call, Fremantle harbour, to come into sight.

The tugboats pushed the ship into place, and it bumped against the wharf, the crew tied ropes in place and shortly afterwards the gangplank was lowered. It was all taking far too long, Emilia wanted to see her husband and the children, their Papa. Rosanna was carrying her mother's suitcase because it was too heavy for Emilia. Anticipation grew into a heart fluttering excitement as they inched their way forward to the opening on the deck.

Giovanni scrunched his eyes up against the reflection of the morning sun on the white ship while he scanned the deck. He had butterflies and sweaty palms, nervous and excited at the same time. There they were, stepping out onto the gangplank after their names had been ticked off the list. Cesare was supporting his Mama around her waist, and she held on tight to the rope railing. Giovanni noticed how frail Emilia appeared. The girls were following close behind concentrating on watching where they were going. Stepping onto the wharf, they were hurriedly shuffled off to the Immigration Hall. Half an hour later, after the formalities were complete, they walked out into the bright sunshine and searched through the faces of the people in the waiting crowd. Giovanni waved his hat high above his head. Emilia gasped at the sight of him, her eyes stung with tears of joy and love. She released a deep breath and a comforting peace flooded over her. Then the children saw their father.

"There he is!" Rosanna squealed, she dropped the cases and ran to him. Cesare did the same.

"Papa, Papa," they called out, and a timid Silvana followed in the wake of her siblings. They nearly knocked Giovanni over in their rush, kneeling down he embraced them in a tangle of hugs and kisses while tears streamed down his face. He couldn't believe how much they'd grown. They excitedly chatted to him, spilling out a multitude of words all over the top of each other, telling him about their voyage and asking him a myriad of questions.

Picking Silvana up, he stood and strode across the wharf with Rosanna and Cesare running along beside him. Reaching Emilia surrounded by abandoned luggage, Giovanni carefully put his daughter down and with open arms welcomed his wife. They stood entwined in each other's arms for a long time.

CHAPTER SEVENTEEN

A New Beginning

"Jack, get a move on mate. We're already losing two days as it is, let's get going," Peter called out as the family reunion unfolded before him.

"Who is Jack?" Emilia asked Giovanni.

"That would be me, my love. It's what Australians call me."

A confused Emilia ran the word over her tongue, *'Jack'*, how strange. The men loaded up the utility with all their worldly goods, Cesare got in with Peter. Emilia, the girls and Giovanni piled into the car with Geoff, and they all set off toward Albany. After they'd stopped for fuel at Bannister, Rosanna sat in the front with Geoff to look for native animals. It wasn't long before Emilia fell asleep on Jack's shoulder and Silvana was sleeping on his lap. His senses tingled at their nearness. Finally, all his dreams of having his family close were coming true. It was a good day, and they were going home.

Peter and Geoff pulled up outside Jack's house. It stood in the midst of long green Kikuyu grass, Jack didn't have time to cut it before they left to go to Perth. The baggage was offloaded, and the two escorts drove away leaving the family on the doorstep. Before they went into the house, Giovanni apologised.

"Emilia, I'm sorry it's not finished yet. It's all a bit primitive, I'm afraid. I hope you won't mind, but I wouldn't change a thing today." Tears glistened in his eyes.

"Me either," she whispered.

He picked her up in front of the door and carried her across the threshold. Balancing her carefully, they edged along the two planks laid across the bearers, where floorboards should have been, to the kitchen beyond. At least that had a concrete floor, solid and sound with a Metters stove against the wall prepared and ready to light. Giovanni struck a match and got the fire going to heat the water in the kettle. He had purchased pantry items and provisions for the week and to make a meal when they arrived home. There was milk, butter, cheese and meat in the Coolgardie safe on the verandah.

"What's this thing, Papa?" Cesare wanted to know. His father explained how the cooler worked.

"It's a wooden frame covered with wire mesh, and see the metal tray on top, we fill it with water. Then one end of the hessian bag goes in the tray to soak up the water, and it makes it wet. When a breeze blows, the air passes through the wet bag and evaporates the water, cooling the air inside the safe. It keeps the food cool to stop it from going bad too quickly. Any excess water from the hessian drips into the tray underneath. Most families without electricity have one of these until they can buy a gas fridge."

Fascinated, Cesare poked a finger in the water and looked inside and outside the frame trying to understand the concept. The children, with arms out, went back and forth across the planks playing a balancing game to entertain themselves without thought of the incompleteness of their new home. The lounge room had no ceiling, and you could see the rafters and tin roof sheeting from inside the house. After their first meal, the children were given a wash, and all of them snuggled together in a double bed on the back verandah. The new surroundings didn't bother them, they chatted a bit but exhausted from the trip fell asleep almost straight away.

Giovanni and Emilia sat by the lamplight talking for a while before walking the plank to their room. Relief and emotion of their reunion bubbled up in Emilia as she lay in her husband's arms, sobbing without control.

While his family slept, Jack got ready to go to work, made his lunch and filled his thermos. He tiptoed into the bedroom and kissed Emilia lightly on the cheek. She stirred. "I'm off to work love. I'll be back tonight around six o'clock. You can spend the day however you like, maybe unpack a few things. I'll help get water heated for baths after I get home and answer any questions you've got. 'Bye, love you."

They had discussed that Giovanni was to go back to work straight away, but Emilia wasn't ready for the sense of loss she felt when he walked out the door. She rolled over in the bed by herself, unsure of what lay ahead. There was a quick knock on the door which burst open and three children piled onto the bed with their mother.

"Mama, we had two spiders in our room. One was skinny with really long legs, and the other one was a fat, ugly and hairy brown spider." Cesare gleefully parted with this information. "We chased them off with the broom." The girls were shuddering with disgust at the recollection of the event. "We didn't kill them though."

"You should be careful, they might be poisonous, it could have been like a *Violino*, for all you know," Emilia admonished.

"Come on, let's have breakfast and go exploring," they urged their mother. "Papa said those posts with the wire running through them are our fences, and that's how much land we have, it's huge." Emilia shooed them off while she got dressed then walked the plank to the kitchen shaking her head at their enthusiasm. Some of which she hoped would rub off on her.

After cleaning up the kitchen and making the beds, they wandered around the moist grassy property. Exploring is what they were doing, the children insisted. They found a little stream with tadpoles and managed to get their shoes, arms and legs wet and dirty while thoroughly enjoying the discovery.

"Why don't the houses here have an upstairs Mama?" Cesare asked. Curious about how different the buildings were from what he was used to seeing.

"I'm not sure, Cesare, I suppose when there is this much flat land they don't need to build two or three storey houses."

"How come they have fences like this Mama?"

"Maybe it's cheaper, or maybe there aren't enough rocks around. We had stone walls and concrete fences at home because of the snow. Maybe it's because it doesn't snow here."

"No snow. Really? Not ever?"

"No, but it's snowing in Italy now because it's winter there."

"And summer here," mused Rosanna.

"I wish I could go up the mountain with Nonno on the cart and get sawdust from Martinelli's sawmill. I loved doing that with him," Cesare's demeanour changed from his previous chirpiness.

"And I want to play with Nonna Silvia," added Silvana.

"I miss my school friends," Rosanna said quietly. Within minutes the children were all teary, and Emilia was saddened by their realisation of what they were missing. Gathering them around her, they stood huddled together crying in the middle of the paddock of this strange new land. Resolving to keep their spirits up, she made a suggestion.

"Let's get cleaned up, and we'll see if there are some ingredients to make 'Jumping Johnnies'?" Three sets of moist eyes looked at their Mama, aware she was trying to make them feel better. They agreed the little doughnuts would definitely help. The afternoon wore on slowly. Clothes were stored in boxes for each of them in their room, and then they took the few toys they had outside to play in the sunshine. Jack surprised them by coming home earlier than they anticipated. The children raced to meet their Papa when they saw him walking down the road toward their house.

"Hello, my family. How was your day?" he asked in English. They looked at him with an odd expression on their faces. Jack translated what he had said and got them to say it back to him. Giggling at the strange words, they repeated them over and over again until they drove their parents to distraction. Emilia looked deeply into her husband's eyes.

"Hello my love," he said tentatively. "How was your day?"

"We have a lot of questions for you," she responded. They discussed Australian spiders, houses, fences and weather patterns over a cup of coffee and some saved doughnuts. Jack stood up from the table ready to go outside.

"I'm sorry for the basic way we have to live for a while, Emilia."

"Stop apologising; we'll manage."

"But I need to explain. I'm going to get the water into the copper to heat for baths. The rainwater can only be used for drinking, cooking and some of the washing, especially during summer. Even though it rains in summer, the tank is too small to waste it for bathwater. I'll have to scoop water out of a hole I've dug for that, but it's brown." She looked confused, the water at home was crystal clear.

"Sorry love, it's clean, but discoloured. When I build a large concrete water tank one day, we'll be able to use it for everything." The children helped scoop water into buckets and watched as Jack lit a fire under the copper to make the water hot. The warm water was carried to the tub in tin buckets to the small shed used as a bathroom, and they took turns to have a bath, in brown water.

"Will we get brown like the Aborigines?" the children asked. They had seen some Aboriginal people at Mt Barker on the way down from Perth.

"No, of course not, but it might stick to you if you don't wash properly," Jack smiled behind his hand, his heart sang with the joy of family. Family, this is what it was all about, having them right here and not missing out on this kind of conversation.

"Tomorrow we are going to town to show you where you will go to school at the convent and you'll meet Sister Angelina who is in charge," Jack said. "School started a few weeks ago, but you will begin on Monday. You will catch a bus down the road in the morning, and we'll show you where to get on the same bus at school in the afternoon. Then you get off at the same place where you get on, and you walk home." He thought it was best to get the children settled into their new routine as soon as possible and had arranged an appointment after school finished.

"Do we have to speak English?" Rosanna asked.

"You will learn it at school, and while you're learning, you can make signs with your hands or use expressions on your face to communicate. It will take a while, but the teacher says children learn quickly. I'll help you with the bit I know, and before long you will be teaching Mama and me English. Look how you were prattling off those sentences today."

"Can I go too?" Silvana looked hopeful.

"Yes," her Papa smiled at her. "They start school here in the year you turn six. You will be six this year, won't you?"

"Yes. Now, I get to go to school, too." Silvana was the only one happy about the whole idea. Rosanna and Cesare were a bit frightened of how they were going to understand what they were supposed to do. A shadow passed over Emilia's heart. She thought Silvana would be home with her for at least another six months, but of course, the school year here was different and started in February, not September.

The school excursion went smoothly, with forms completed to enrol the three children and arrangements made for travel on the bus to start on Monday. They went shopping for pencils, a sharpener and a ruler each. Their travel cases would do to take their lunch and any other things they would need.

At 10 o'clock on Sunday morning a car pulled up outside the house and tooted. Geoff jumped out and called for Jack to get his family ready to go to the beach. He had some bathers for the girls and said Cesare could wear a pair of shorts. They gathered some towels and a blanket to take and packed some cheese, bread and a few pieces of fruit.

Jack lifted three excited children into the back of the utility, ready to go. The beach was a novelty they had heard about from their Papa and Nunzio. They'd seen beaches from the ship, but that wasn't the same as walking on the sand or going in the sea. Emilia emerged from the front door, wearing a sundress she hadn't used since before the war. Jack took a second look and smiled. Geoff introduced his tall and elegant wife, Olive, to Emilia and the Preston's got into the car.

"You look very pretty Mrs Nostrini," he gave her a quick hug.

"Thank you, '*Jack*'," she responded with a smile in her eyes.

"Let me help you," he said, and he knelt down with one knee bent to use as a step and put his hand up for her to hold while she climbed onto the utility tray. Emilia took his hand as she placed her sandalled foot on his leg to climb in with the children. Giovanni was pleased she was wearing her wedge heeled shoes he'd bought for her in Milan all those years ago. The healing balm of her presence nurtured his soul, and he felt whole again.

They bounced along the gravel road to town jostled around in the back of the ute and enjoyed the fun of it. The sun shone brightly, and a gentle breeze blew as they drove along York Street in the centre of Albany, past Dog Rock and along Middleton Road to the beach. Tall Norfolk pines lined the grassed area where they found some shade to settle under and spread out their towels and a blanket.

The children timidly approached the water, but it didn't take long for them to splash each other and jump over the waves. They had a snack and rest before wading out into the water nearly up to their waists and spent much of the afternoon in the water. Olive helped them build a big sandcastle with the wet white beach sand, and they decorated it with shells and seaweed. Emilia thoroughly enjoyed the time spent relaxing with her husband. Tired and hungry in the late afternoon everyone packed up and drove home, sunburnt but happy.

On Monday morning it was time to get the children ready for school. Cesare complained because his back was red raw and hurt when he put his shirt on. Jack had gone to work a bit dubious about leaving them to find their way to school on their own. Emilia was to walk to the bus stop with them and make sure they got on all right. The bus pulled up on time and off they went. Three olive-skinned, brown-eyed and dark-haired children clung to each other after they got off the bus and went to the Grade One classroom to wait for school to start.

Emilia cried all the way back to the house after they drove away in the big orange school bus on that first morning. She made a cup of tea and tried to control the sadness threatening to overwhelm her, she was completely and utterly alone. The clothes from the weekend needed washing, and Jack had filled the copper with water and lit it before he left, so there was warm water to use. She decided it would be best to get busy and stop wallowing in self-pity. Soon freshly washed clothes were pegged onto the post and wire clothesline and flapped in the breeze and sunshine. It was much better than the short line on the balcony at home. She felt a bit better and decided to do her housework and make something for the children to have to eat when they got home from school.

At nine o'clock when the bell rang, the students lined up beside the bench seat where three Italian children were sitting. They stared at the newcomers curiously. The Nun clapped her hands loudly, and they all immediately hushed and stood up straight. Their teacher reached for Silvana and took her by the hand, then indicated to Rosanna and Cesare to follow them to the back of the line. She told them this is where they should be and even though they couldn't understand the words, they realised that's what they were meant to do.

Everyone walked in and sat at a desk. The Nun pointed and told them to sit down at the three empty spaces at the front of the class-room. Silvana clung to Rosanna, terrified, so they sat together at one of the desks. Cesare sat at the other one next to a girl with glasses and two long plaits. The roll was called, and when the Nun called Cesare, as in Julius *Caesar,* sniggers could be heard from the children sitting behind them. The Nun looked up and glared at them, and the room went silent again. Rosanna towered over the others and felt conspicuous and embarrassed.

They were given a writing pad marked with pale blue lines and had to rule up the page and write their name at the top. The Nun showed them how to copy letters and words onto their page from the black-board. At recess they watched the children from the verandah, two girls came to talk to them, but when they didn't get an answer, they ran off to play. At least they knew how to line up after the bell rang, they got that right this time and again after lunch. Silvana fell asleep when it was rest time in the afternoon, and Cesare sat bolt upright, so his sunburnt back didn't touch the chair, it hurt too much.

Rosanna was given a reading book about a dog called Nip, and a cat called Fluff to take home to practice the letters and words and share it with her brother and sister. Mama or Papa had to sign a small flap glued on the front page to say they had done their reading at home. At least that's what Rosanna thought they were supposed to do from her interpretation of the sign language used by their teacher. The end of the day couldn't come quick enough. They found their bus, got on and were happy to look for the road where they would get off. What a relief to go home.

The afternoon dragged on, and several times Emilia walked to the front gate to look down the road to see if the children were on their way back. Finally, they came. They ran to her when they saw her in the distance. It all came out, what they did, where they sat, about the others in their class and the Nun. Emilia was a bit daunted by it all, but most particularly by the reading book – how were they to help their children when they couldn't read it themselves. Jack would work out what to do because he was the problem solver in the family.

CHAPTER EIGHTEEN

Struggles

LONELINESS ENGULFED EMILIA. THE SUMMER days stretched out before her seemingly endless. Thankfully, Lia was a faithful companion, and Emilia often talked to the family's pet dog. It was difficult trying to be bright and happy for her family when they were around. During the day, Emilia would often cry without reserve. Lia would come and snuggle up beside her, aware of her emotional distress.

The highlight of the day was when the children arrived home from school, but it only lasted a short while until they ran off to play at a neighbours' house. They had a tyre and rope swing hanging from a tree, and they played hide and seek at the sandpit. You didn't need any language skills to play those games, and they managed to communicate with each other quite well.

Emilia was pleased with how they'd settled in, Silvana was going ahead in leaps and bounds with her English. She was the one helping them with their reading books, telling her brother and sister it was Nip and Fluff, not Neep and Floof like they were pronouncing it with Italian alphabet sounds. Jack was working long hours to earn as much money as he could. When he arrived back at Peter's house, he was expected to work in the garden, often in the dark, before coming home.

Letters from home seemed to be few and far between. Emilia would religiously write to her family and Giovanni to his. They would give them to Teresa to post when she went to the post office once a fortnight. Mail was delivered to the letterboxes lined up at the end of the street for all the houses in the Robinson Road area, and the children checked the mail on their way home from school. They took turns to have a look and were sad when it was another day without a letter from Italy. It hurt them to see the hope in their Mama's eyes turn dull again, and they would make extra effort to cheer her up.

Before lunch, Emilia had a nagging desire to check the letterbox herself. She didn't want to wait until the afternoon, the mail was delivered mid-morning, and she was desperate for news from home. She wandered down the long gravel road after she had a cup of tea, Lia was asleep in the sunshine and didn't follow her.

Not far from the corner, a bobtail goanna warmed itself on the road. When it felt the vibrations from Emilia's footsteps, it turned and moved toward the bush across her path. She paused in the shade of a gum tree and waited. Teresa came across to collect her mail and then went to the Nostrini box and pulled out a blue envelope and tucked it in her apron pocket. Emilia was stunned. Surely Teresa couldn't be so cruel to steal her letters from home, but she'd seen it with her own eyes.

Upset, and angry, Emilia decided to return home without approaching her neighbour. She would let her husband do that. It occurred to her there might have been more mail taken before today. The longing for that letter burnt into her being for the rest of the day, most of which was spent with hot tears streaming down her sad face. Jack was furious when he found out but with his usual sense of decency, decided he would speak to the mailman first.

Once he discovered other overseas letters had been delivered but not received by them, he stormed down the road and railed with disgust at the goings-on. He demanded the return of any mail that had been confiscated and was given a small bundle, dated over many months. This erosion of trust was never mended, and Jack was polite from then on, but only because he had no other choice. The proffered excuse of helping his wife overcome her homesickness was not valid; it made things worse. It hurt that one of their own would treat them like this.

The delight of seeing her mother's handwriting, and reading the news crammed onto the thin blue paper, was only marred by the deceit of her neighbour. There were letters from Nino, Giuliana and Carla. Carla happily announced her marriage to Nunzio would take place in the spring and Emilia was surprised to learn they had applied to come to the Barossa Valley in South Australia. Nunzio's experience in the vineyard at Negri Wines stood him in good stead for being accepted into a job in the wine region not far from Adelaide.

Emilia smiled at Carla's comment that they would be able to catch up. Obviously, she was ignorant of the distances between cities and towns in Australia. Should she make Carla aware of the separation anxiety she experienced being so far away from her family? After she gave it some thought she realised because Carla had a positive disposition she would cope much better. Probably best not to say anything at all. Her reply would focus on the excitement of the upcoming wedding.

Every Thursday a man from Drew Robinson & Co. would come and collect the shopping lists from residences in the area for deliveries on Friday. Emilia would put together a list of things she needed and pass it on to Teresa each Wednesday to be translated into English. Often items would be crossed out as 'not available', Emilia became quite confused when she realised they then had to buy those things like butter and cheese from Teresa. If they wanted fresh vegetables from the garden Jack tended at their place, they were made to pay for them. They bought milk from their neighbours every day, and it was Rosanna's job to walk down with the milk can to get it. If she went too early and had to wait, Teresa would make her weed the garden, but Rosanna got smart and when she saw the cows wander down to the dairy, then and only then, would she get her container and go collect the milk.

Money was tight, and with many expenses to cover, it seemed like they were on a merry-go-round. Further building on the house was regularly put on hold as unexpected costs had to be paid for first. Jack was exhausted most of the time from the burden of constant work and worry. At least they were healthy, and on those days when things looked bleak, Jack and Emilia would hear their children laughing and playing happily together. It was the encouragement they needed to know it was worth the struggle. Emilia received a child endowment payment of fifteen shillings per week paid by the Government. It wasn't much, but it did help.

Olive Preston had taken to Emily, as she called her, and they became close friends. They valued the time they spent together, whether at each other's home or on the occasions when Geoff insisted they do something special. On one Sunday morning, they all piled in the car and headed off to the Porongorup Ranges to climb Castle Rock, and have a picnic. Olive recommended Emily for a job to take care of Matron Grocock's children at their home and to do some ironing and cleaning for her. Emily took the job. She got the bus into town in the morning and returned on the school bus in the afternoon. Sometimes Mrs Northcott and Mrs Niven were on the bus as well. They were friendly and would try to talk to her. Emily earned enough money to help tide them over, and it gave her something to do to break the boredom. The children were well-behaved, and Mrs Grocock's mother was kind to her when she came to visit, even though they couldn't communicate with each other. Emily couldn't thank Olive enough for helping her, it made a big difference in many ways.

The children at St Joseph's convent school took the shy newcomers under their wing and encouraged them to play at recess and lunchtime. Rosie, Ces and Sil had become their adapted names in the playground. 'Ces' – was said like seez, and Cesare like seeza.

Ces put up his hand in class before the bell rang. The Nun looked at him and nodded.

"Please Sister, my Mama wants me to go and get my head cut at lunchtime."

The children in the classroom started laughing, the teacher was confused, and then the cloud lifted.

"Oh, you mean you need a 'haircut'," she smiled at his mistake. "Of course you can go, thank you for remembering to ask before you leave the school grounds." Often after that incident, Cesare would cop a friendly teasing by the other boys who would ask him if he needed his head cut today.

Once a week Emilia would give Rosie money to go to the butchers and buy some meat. It was close to the school so there was time to do that and still catch the bus home. On one occasion while they waited to be served, a lady in front of them asked Mr Hunter if he had any parsley. He apologised and said it was all gone. It was Rosie's turn to be served next.

"I want six lamb chops, please." Then plucking up courage she asked, "Do you want some more parsley to sell? We've got heaps of it at home." If he bought it, she would be proud to help the family out.

"Mmm, I did run out today, didn't I? The ladies like to put it in the white sauce when they cook corned beef. Sure, how about you bring me some tomorrow?" The next day Rosie went over to the butcher shop before school with a large bunch of fresh parsley. Mr Hunter was impressed and agreed to the arrangement; he gave her some coins and thanked her. Emilia was proud of her daughter and a few months later gave Rosie a new challenge.

"Mr Hunter, Mama wants to know if it would be all right to have some meat instead of money."

"Sure, come back after school and collect it before you get on the bus. We don't want it to go off sitting in your case all day."

"Thank you. I'll see you later," Rosie called over her shoulder on the way out. He watched her go with a little skip in her step and he smiled, they had it tough, and he was happy to help. He was very generous and on those days her small case was full of meat.

Shopping list day was approaching, and Emily felt uneasy about giving her list to Teresa again. She determined it was time to change some things.

"Jack, I want to give the shopping list to the man from Drew Robinson's myself."

"Why?"

"I just want to."

"Okay, it might be a bit tricky to get the words right in English. And we have to use ounces and pounds for things that have to be weighed."

"We'll learn, I can ask Olive to help me."

They arranged for him to ride his bike down to their place the following Thursday. Lia chased the motorbike and frightened him, but Emily indicated she would tie her up next time. She was rapt on Friday when the delivery had everything on the list she'd ordered.

Their red wine was delivered in a small barrel by train from the Luisini Winery in Perth and had to be collected from the railway station. Some other continental items had to come from an importer in Perth as well.

CHAPTER NINETEEN

Renzo from Boffetto

A TALL MAN WITH STRIKING features stood on the pier, his demeanour purposeful and confident. At 23, his adventurous spirit had him boarding the ship *'Roma'* at Genoa. He'd found it difficult to say goodbye to his family in the tiny village of Boffetto just out of Sondrio. He hadn't anticipated how hard it would be to leave his parents and siblings, but he knew it was what he wanted to do. The opportunity to immigrate to Australia had caught his attention, and he decided to go. All his belongings were packed into a small wooden case made by his brother Michele. He had an Australian £5 note in his pocket, the only money he possessed. Renzo, as his family called him, had his passport ready. It was May 14, 1952 and Aldo Lorenzo Scamozzi embarked on a journey across the ocean to Fremantle.

The day before they reached their destination, after three weeks at sea, the second-class passengers were made to line up outside the bathroom. Staff ticked off names as they were sent in. Aldo was next.

"Right, you there, strip off and get in the tub, and wash yourself thoroughly, and wash all your clothes too."

"You mean I have to get into that?"

"Yes sir, it's what everyone from down below has to do."

"Only the second-class passengers, so why is that?"

"Not my place to say, sir. Just do as you are asked if you want to get off this boat tomorrow."

The bath was full of hot green foul smelling water. Aldo sank down into the disinfectant solution and scrubbed himself. His other clothes had already been washed in it a few days earlier. He groaned when he redressed and discovered they'd all shrunk, his pant legs and shirt sleeves now exposed his ankles and revealed his wrists.

On Friday, June 6 the ship berthed, and he walked down the gangplank. He approached the immigration desk, Aldo Scamozzi's paperwork was stamped as approved and he ventured out to a bus waiting to transfer him and others to Australia Hotel in the city. During that week he canvassed the Perth City Council for a job, which was not forthcoming. The promised work was limited and not easy for an immigrant to find, contrary to what they'd been told in Italy. Young and undaunted by not finding work as a bricklayer, he took a job with the West Australian Government Railways in a shifting gang.

Aldo wiped the perspiration from his forehead with the clean rag he used as a handkerchief. The train ride on the Prospector rattled along the railway line across red and barren terrain through to Merredin and Burracoppin. He disembarked at the station and was approached by a WAGR supervisor. The middle-aged man stretched out his hand and shook Aldo's firmly. He wondered how he knew he was the new employee but then realised only a few passengers had come this far. The others knew where they were going or someone had come to pick them up.

"Good afternoon," Aldo greeted him with his simple language skills.

"Welcome to the goldfields son. My name's Jim," he said slowly. "You'll get used to the heat and flies out here in time. Come on down to the pub, mate. We'll get you settled for the night, and we'll knock back a nice cold beer." Nodding in reply, he followed him to a two storey building on the corner. It was a plain building with a wide verandah and tin roof with rusty patches here and there.

After taking his case to his room and washing up, he went downstairs to the bar and gratefully accepted the offered drink.

"So, you'll begin working on the new line to Bullfinch starting tomorrow at the camp. Your workday begins at 8.30 in the morning until 4.30 in the afternoon with a break for lunch. It gets up to 113 degrees Fahrenheit on some days. Make sure you drink plenty of water and keep your head covered. We've had the occasional Italian workers here, and they tied knots in the corner of their hankies, wet them and put them on their heads. You can do that if you want, it's up to you, and you can look forward to an ice-cold beer at the end of the day with the other fellows."

"Thank you," Aldo responded by nodding his head. He wasn't sure of what the man had said, but he'd work it out.

Aldo was efficient, reliable and hard working. They made camp, rows of red stained white canvas tents lined up one after the other. One morning Aldo pushed the tent flap aside and stood outside. A thorny devil scuttled past with its odd jerky movements and disappeared into a clump of spinifex. This country was noticeably different from his hometown. Vastness beyond belief, a solitary stunted tree in the distance was the only break on the horizon. Red dirt stretched as far as the eye could see with cloudless skies and unrelenting sunshine every day.

"Gidday Aldo, you sleep okay?" one of the gang asked.

"Yes, thank you."

"I got up early today to take photos of the sunrise. Would you like me to take a photo of you there? Just for memories sake, you know, for in the future. Not every day an Italian gets to be out here, hey?"

"Yes, please, that would be good." Aldo straightened up while the fellow focussed the camera and took the picture.

"It'll be a while before we get it back, it's gotta go to Merredin to be developed. As soon as I get it, I'll pass it on to you." Aldo smiled, pleased with himself that he understood. He studied his English-Italian dictionary by the light of his Tilly lamp every evening before going to bed. The next day he'd checked with someone about the pronunciation, and practise the words. Now he managed to communicate much better with his peers.

He sent the photo to his family, only to discover sometime later it caused his mother a great deal of distress. Not a blade of grass, no stand of trees and not a hill in sight, let alone a mountain. She'd cried for weeks.

It was a nomadic lifestyle. The gang had moved further south-east and worked near the townsite of Widgiemooltha in the extreme inland summer heat for four months. The supervisor offered Aldo a more responsible role with a higher rate of pay as a main ganger, but he declined. He'd had enough of this lifestyle after 18 months, and his cousin, Joe Scamozzi had written to him and suggested he come to Albany in the South West.

The Prospector pulled away from the platform, Aldo looked out the window and watched spinifex tumble across the dusty red plains blown along by a strong wind. The miles melted away, and eventually, the landscape began to change, leaving the goldfields behind. Trees with straight, stark white trunks crowned with a canopy of grey-green eucalyptus leaves glistened in the morning sunlight.

Farmland stretched for miles with green crops growing on either side of the train tracks. Passengers alighted at stops along the way. Brick and tile houses emerged on the outskirts of towns, the tin sheds and asbestos shacks left behind in the wilderness. Aldo changed trains at Northam railway station and boarded the Albany Progress. It rattled and rocked all night with stops at each siding and station along the way. Early the next day, he shaved and washed his face in the tight confines of the men's toilet at the end of the passenger car. As they approached their destination, he saw the stunning Princess Royal Harbour shrouded in a light mist.

The water was perfectly still, not a breath of air disturbed it except for the wake of a large white bird with black wingtips tucked into its side and sporting a strange looking long pink bill. Picking up his case, he left the carriage. A welcome autumn chill in the air refreshed his senses. Aldo approached the driver of a waiting taxi and asked him to take him 'somewhere to sleep'. He entered the boarding house on the corner of Collie and Duke Streets and made a booking. The next morning someone came in an old Austin truck to pick him up and take him to his pre-arranged job. Aldo met Jack Nostrini. They shook hands and drove to the building site together - and there began a life-long friendship.

Aldo's accommodation provided in Parade Street wasn't much better than his tent at the outback campsite; a rusty tin shed with a dirt floor not even big enough to swing a cat in, as they say. A rickety old iron bed with a kapok mattress took up most of the space. A small Companion gas burner stove sat on a makeshift table. An Aussie long drop toilet beside the shed was the extent of his ablution provision. It was bitterly cold in winter and uncomfortably hot in summer. His landlord, Peter Caraffa, employed him to work on his house near the Woollen Mills. Soon after his arrival, Aldo arranged to buy a block of land in Earl Street from Peter for £250. He spent all his spare time clearing the bush ready to prepare a level building site. Most of his pay had to cover his rent and payments on the land, with a bit of cash left for food and other essential items. Mr Walker, the real estate agent, made the arrangements for the legal purchase of the land in Earl Street for £300; an extra £50 had been added to the cost for clearing of the property. The agent was surprised to learn Aldo was, in fact, the one who had cleared it and was now expected to pay for the job he had done himself.

The day was warm, and the sea breeze hadn't come in yet. Aldo swiped at the sweat on his brow with his sleeve. Dr Fitz's father went through the front verandah door and let the flyscreen bang closed. Aldo looked up.

"Come on Aldo. Lunch is ready. You've been at it for hours, and now it's time for a break."

"I can't come into the house."

"Why not? Mrs Fitz has made us ham and salad sandwiches and got a cold beer in the fridge. She'll be upset if you don't come in."

"But I'm all dirty and...,"

"Doesn't matter, come on. And leave those boots on, no need to take them off."

Aldo was embarrassed but grateful for their companionship. Over lunch, he told them about a lady he met who couldn't start her car last night. He was on his way back from town and wanted to help her. After he checked everything he thought it could be, he realised she'd flooded the engine. He explained to them, waving his hands around in the air, how he turned the key on in the ignition; put his foot down hard on the accelerator and away it went. The lady was thankful, especially when she knew it wasn't a mechanical issue and drove off in her blue Ford. Aldo appreciated the meal with the couple, a warm sense of welcoming kindness enveloped him. They shared lunch and conversation every day while he worked for them.

Since he couldn't afford to build a house on the Earl Street block, Aldo spoke to Peter about a block of land in Elphinstone Road to put up a shed. It wasn't subdivided yet, but they allowed him to build it with a proposed purchase agreement to be arranged. He built a seven by ten-foot shack to live in with a dream to develop it into a proper house one day. The Nostrini children loved to see Aldo when he came to their place, or, they would run up the hill to visit him. He championed them with stories and played games. An infatuated Rosanna, eleven at the time, was quite taken with this young Italian man whom they saw regularly.

Aldo saved up and bought a 125*cc* motorbike from Cranbrook. He loved it, loved the freedom to transport himself around the place and have the wind blow in his face, it was invigorating. He rode down the hill to where he would be picked up for work, but Peter Caraffa drove straight on by, even though Aldo could be seen from the road.

"Joe, what's going on? Why didn't he stop?"

"Blowed if I know. Mongrel."

"What'll we do?"

"I'm not going to work for him ever again, that's what." Joe shrugged and started walking back home.

Aldo took some of his tools on his bike and looked for some little jobs around town. A few days later he plucked up the courage to confront Peter.

"Peter, I want the money you owe me for all the work I've done."

"Oh, right, just a minute." He walked out the door to the other room.

"Here you are." Peter handed him a letter and indicated where he should sign it. Aldo read the letter and looked up in controlled disgust.

"You expect me to sign this?"

"Yeah, then we'll be okay with everything." Peter was surprised Aldo understood the document.

"No, we won't. I am not signing to say 'I'm satisfied with the arrangement to exonerate you from any obligation', you owe me for the work I've done. You pay me, or I'll take this to the Arbitration Court to deal with it on my behalf."

Aldo remained calm, but he was furious with the man. Peter didn't know his previous employee was aware of such things. He left the room again and returned with an envelope of £220 cash this time. Although it wasn't much for his ten months labour, at least Aldo got something. The threat was a bluff because he wouldn't have followed it through but at least he stood up for himself and got something back.

A few months later Peter told him the partner of the block on Elphinstone Road wouldn't agree to the purchase of the property. Aldo had to leave his shed behind and was given shelter on the verandah of the Nostrini family home. Jack was not impressed with the treatment any of them had received from the hands of the Caraffa couple but what could he do, he still owed them money and continued to work for Peter, although it irked him.

CHAPTER TWENTY

Reckoning

THIS CHILD NEVER SETTLED. EMILY was sure the other babies had not been so active. Matron Grocock's children were off to kindergarten and school, and Emily missed their sweet smiles and company. She and Jack decided they would have another baby now they could manage better financially. Another jolt to her ribcage made Emily gasp, Doctor Martin had confirmed her due date was Christmas Day, 1955.

There was a knock at the door, and a neighbour stood on the doorstep with a covered dish of food. Emily smiled and asked her to come in. No longer embarrassed by the lack of floorboards and their humble abode, she waddled over to the stove and put the kettle on. Mrs Northcott sat at the kitchen table for a morning cuppa with her friend. Emily had been devastated to learn her neighbours had been told by Teresa, when she first arrived in Albany, that she didn't want visitors. Loneliness and mistreatment compounded the anxiety she'd felt in those early days. When they all caught the bus into town together, they had the opportunity to get to know each other.

She felt quite sick most days lately. The local women volunteered to help out with an occasional meal. Emily's heart swelled with an appreciation of their kindness; these ladies were her friends. That reminded her of Carla's letter, she got it out of the drawer and sat down to answer it, but first, she reread it.

October 29, 1955

My dear friend, Emilia

I hope this finds you well and happy. I thought of you today on your wedding anniversary, and I'm sorry I haven't been in touch before now; we've been through a lot lately. You will notice this letter has been posted from Italy and not in Australia. Our plans to live and work in the Barossa Valley in South Australia didn't work out for us. The children missed my parents so much they were miserable. I confess, I too, cried many tears for my Mama, but that wasn't the main reason we came home.

Poor Nunzio tried hard to persevere, and although the work was easy, he couldn't cope with the vineyard owners and workers. He started to have nightmares again, prompted by hearing German all day. We had no idea the wine growing area there was mostly settled by German people, not that any of them were unkind or had anything to do with the war, but it caused too many reminders for Nunzio.

So we packed up and came back, Papa was relieved to see us walk up the road and ran to greet us. Mama is excited she has another grandchild on the way and especially pleased we'll be here for her to know and spoil it. I say 'it' because I am sure there will only be one baby this time. There are no twins in Nunzio's family thank goodness. Once was enough, mind you, I wouldn't want to be without my precious son and daughter. Antonio is becoming more like Raph as he grows up and is a blessing to us all.

Carla had written several more pages of her usual ramblings. Emily smiled at the memory of her friend and wrote a short note in reply ready to put in the post to Italy.

Olive, Geoff and baby Carol turned up on Saturday afternoon with a huge Christmas tree. It had become Geoff's custom to deliver a tree on Christmas Eve each year. The family enjoyed decorating the Albany woolly bush with baubles and homemade paper chains, and they all shared a meal together. This year, with Emily's due date the next day, Olive had made all the food and brought it with her. It was a joyous time for them, the Preston's had tried for years to have a child with no success, until now. A year ago Emily had given Olive a parsley plant out of her garden and told her to plant it at home – then she would become a mother. Initially Olive scoffed at the idea of such nonsense, but she laughed out loud when she fell pregnant not long afterwards.

Everyone waited in anticipation for the birth of the baby. The older children wanted to find out if they would have a brother or sister, and with not long to go Emily was ready to be free of the burdensome cargo she bore. Christmas Day dawned bright and sunny, but no baby arrived. Boxing Day came and went, and on December 27, 1955, St Stephen's Day, they welcomed a wriggly Steven John Nostrini, an Australian born son and brother. It was a relief and delight for Emily, and the months flew by now with the busyness of a young baby in the home.

A bold and determined Rosie called in at the Woollen Mills to let them know she wanted a job. She'd had enough of school and felt it was more important to earn some money for the family. The manager called in the foreman, Mr Dawson, who told her they needed a new worker for a particular machine but employees had to be 14 to work there. Rosie said she was 14, even though she'd only turn 13 on her birthday in a couple of month's time. She got the job straight away and took home a pay packet to her parents each week. When there was work available on Saturday mornings, she took it because the pay was higher than the usual rate. Rosie was pleased to see her Mum happy and more settled than ever before.

Finally, Jack was debt free with no more obligations to his neighbour and employer. After handing over the final sum of money, Jack left the yard with a spring in his step and a sense of freedom he hadn't felt before. He felt good, very good. However, they had a long way to go before they were comfortable and many goals yet to achieve.

Aldo had begun to join the family for meals because Jack couldn't see the sense of him cooking his own when he lived on their doorstep. He provided more than his fair share of grocery items and pitched in to help out around the place. Jack wrote to a cousin in Italy to see if she was interested in coming to Australia to marry Aldo, but she declined. A serious discussion took place between the two men. Aldo asked if he could wait for Rosie to grow up and marry her, he knew she liked him and might fall in love with him one day. Jack insisted that it could only happen if it was what Rosie wanted. As long as he understood she was under no obligation to marry him, he could wait. Aldo agreed.

Aldo asked Mr Walker, the real estate agent, for a job reference. He intended to approach George Hodgson, who owned a building company, to apply for work. When he did, George decided the best idea was to let him do some bricklaying and see how he went. Aldo spent the morning on his own, working with only a trowel and spirit level, and he built a perfectly level neat wall and got the job straight away.

A loud saw buzzed in the background and made it hard for Jack to hear his instructions, but he was pleased to be in this new work environment. When Bruno Rizzi delivered timber to one of Peter Caraffa's worksites, he'd asked Jack if he would like a job at his sawmill in Narrikup. He welcomed the opportunity now he could take it on, although he did have to leave early in the morning and it was often late when he got home. The work was arduous and could be dangerous.

The logs were trucked to the mill, and the workers loaded the tree trunks onto the rack where they would be fed through a double saw to remove the bark. Once the four sides were taken off, they were left with clean timber. The jarrah or karri would be sliced to suit the orders they had to fill. Most were railway sleepers for a large government contract they'd received, other timber was for construction sites and mill ends were cut up for sale as firewood.

Life was busy for Emily with a veggie patch, milking cow and chooks as they call chickens in Australia but she still called them her *gallina*. She waited patiently every night for her husband to come home. They spent some family time together on the weekends. Their sons and daughters were growing up, little Steven had already turned one. He was walking now and was a busy little boy who always kept himself occupied. Emily enjoyed his toddler stage and was content with life. She still missed her family but getting their regular letters was a highlight of collecting the mail, and she enjoyed writing back with all the changes they experienced.

March 4, 1957

Dearest Mama, Papa and family,

Today is a public holiday in Australia, so we packed up a picnic and went to Frenchman Bay with the Preston's for a few hours. It's rare for us to enjoy such luxury. This beach is protected from the wind with shady peppermint trees and grass underneath to sit on. The water is a sparkling clear turquoise blue. We went for a swim in the bay, and I played on the white sand with Steven. He built a big castle for such a little boy. Cesare and Silvana climbed around the granite rocks looking for small crabs or other sea life caught in tidal pools. Rosie and Aldo walked along the beach chatting to each other. It was good for the soul, especially since I've been feeling a little unwell lately.

I woke up a few weeks ago with plans to do a myriad of chores but ended up trotting out to the toilet several times. I thought I had a tummy upset, but it turns out we are having another baby. This one is due in October, and I wish you were here Mama and Papa. It does make me sad to know you haven't seen Steven and now this baby will not get to meet you either. Anyway, it will be nice for him to have a younger brother or sister.

Giovanni heard about an opportunity to own a hundred acre property for free but with a condition to clear a certain amount of land within a specified period. He put our name down after checking I was okay with it first. We were allocated a block in Jackson Road, not far from Bruno and Bruna Rizzi's place and it has the right feel about it. Bruno is a short but strong man of the land and Bruna is homely to look at and has a big heart. I can talk to her about anything. These people have become good friends, and if we have to move, it would be good to live closer to them. It takes about forty minutes to get there from our place in Elphinstone Road.

I'll let you know more about it soon. It doesn't take very long to fill up one of these aerogramme letters even though I've written my words as small as possible. I can't even write under the stamp as they did during the war because it's printed on the paper.

I love you and miss you every day, but you are in my heart and my memories. I cherish that most of all.

Your loving daughter and sister, Emilia

The land at Narrikup was covered in shrubs and trees. Every weekend Jack would attack the bush on the property with a crosscut saw, mostly by himself, but when he had a volunteer to help, they would use the big double-handled saw. It made the task easier and quicker. The logs were taken to Bruno's sawmill to be cut into planks for a house on the property in the future. It would be a bigger house than where they were living now, but the land had to be cleared first.

Some of the timber was exchanged for dressed floorboards, and Emily finally got the floor in her living room. After Jack hit the last nail into the final board, the family hooted and clapped in celebration. Jack and Emily christened the floor with a waltz, and then they all sat down for a picnic, careful not to spill any food and stain the new timbers.

Jack came in the back door whistling a tune and holding a bunch of daisies he'd picked from a bush near the front gate. Looking up

Emily stopped stirring the pot on the stove. She smiled at him, a little miffed by his unusual behaviour.

"Come on love, take that apron off. We're going to the pictures." His grin widened at the look she gave him.

"What, now? Don't be silly it's nearly dinner time."

"Everything's all arranged, go and put a cardigan on and maybe bring your coat."

"We can't Jack, what about the children? And dinner isn't finished cooking yet."

"Rosie and Aldo will take care of it all. Maybe put these in some water first."

"Why are you acting so strange? What's going on?" She turned the tap on and filled a glass for the flowers.

"I got a raise, and we're going to enjoy just being the two of us. Soon we won't get the chance for a long time." Shrugging and shaking her head, Emily collected her warm clothing and followed him outside. He pulled up the motorbike and placed a folded blanket on the rear part of the seat.

"We're going on that thing?"

"Yes, we are." He laughed at the novelty of her reactions. "Come on, just sit side-saddle here; otherwise, you won't be able to hold onto me." Emily did what he said and with her baby bump out of the way she could just reach around him.

"This is ridiculous."

They arrived at the Empire picture theatre in time for the end of the newsreel. The 20th Century Fox emblem hit the screen with its unique drum roll music, and the movie started. Holding hands like teenagers and sharing a tub of popcorn, the couple took sidelong glances at each other before they started laughing.

"This is ridiculous," Emily repeated, "but it is fun, and you're right we should just enjoy ourselves." At intermission, they went to the cafe next door to the theatre and got a hot cup of coffee. Jack became serious then.

"Emily, it occurred to me today that we're happy here. Albany is our home, and our lives have changed for the better, wouldn't you agree?"

"I would, even though it hasn't been easy, it keeps getting better all the time."

"Let's become Australian citizen's then? What do you think about that?"

"I think I'm glad you asked and didn't just bring home the forms and started filling them out."

"Well, actually...,"

"You didn't! You did, I can tell. You've got the forms, haven't you?"

"Yes, I do, but I haven't done anything with them. I know it has to be a joint decision and we can take time to think about it."

"I'm happy about it if that's what you want to do. It's different here, but it's a good life. Now I have a question for you, do you like the name 'Nadia'? I like hearing it in the movie, maybe we can use it if we have a girl. What do you think about that?"

Nothing about the waiting room was comfortable. The stark white walls and medical charts looked harsh, and there were no magazines or children's books on the table. The couple sat bolt upright on the straight-backed wooden chairs. Their daughter sat on her mother's knee and played with the gold cross she wore around her neck. A white-capped nurse came in and tapped her clipboard with a black biro.

"The doctor will see you now," she announced looking directly at them. She ushered them into the office and closed the door on her way out.

"Mr and Mrs Rizzi, I'm sorry to have to confirm your little girl is deaf. All the tests prove she was born with minimal hearing." Bruna's suspicions were now a reality. The doctor droned on about how a hearing aid might or might not help, and surgery wasn't an option, but arrangements for sign language and lip reading lessons could be arranged. Bruno sat as still as a statue, and neither parent could think clearly, let alone ask questions.

"So, we can discuss the options at length once you've got past the shock of today's news. We'll make an appointment for a few weeks time, shall we?" He stood up. Bruno stood to leave.

"Thank you, Doctor," he said, and Bruna followed him out to the car.

"Can we go to Emily and Jack's please?" Bruna looked forlorn.

"Yes, of course."

The coffee cups on the dining room table sat untouched while the whole episode was revisited. Discussion about Dina's lack of response to loud noises and not attempting to say any words were obvious signs but they thought she might be a late bloomer. Bruna began to cry. Emily held her hand, and both men moved away from the table and left the room.

"I don't understand this because we don't have any deafness in the family that I know of, my poor little Dina. Not being able to hear is going to make life very hard for her. We should have done something about it sooner I suppose. Although from what the doctor said, it probably wouldn't have made any difference. And what about the baby I'm carrying? Will it be all right?"

"Don't worry about what you don't know, Bruna. Look at Dina, she manages very well." They watched her sitting on the floor playing with Silvana who helped her to dress a doll. "I think she'll surprise you when she gets older at how well she'll cope."

"Mama," a sleepy voice called out from the bedroom. Emily went to pick Steven up from his afternoon nap, thankful he was listening and learning but she felt compassion for her friend who wouldn't hear those words from Dina. Six months later, Bruno and Bruna had a son. He was profoundly deaf.

Nadia Nostrini was born on October 24, 1957. Emily was delighted to have a daughter, and they used the name she had chosen from the movie. Their family was complete, and both parents were thrilled with her safe arrival.

CHAPTER TWENTY-ONE

I Do

THE BED CREAKED WHEN A frustrated Rosie sat down on it heavily.

"He's going to the pictures, again. I bet he's meeting someone there."

"What did you say?" Silvana asked, looking at her sister from across the room.

"Nothing, I was talking to myself."

"Oh, okay." And Sil went back to what she was doing.

"Is that all you can say?"

"What do you want me to say then?"

"It's Aldo, he's gone off again tonight. Do you think he's got a girlfriend? He must have or why else would he keep going out during the week."

"No, he just likes going to the pictures. Are you jealous?"

"Not if he doesn't have a girlfriend, I'm not."

"Rosie's in love with Aldo, Rosie's in love with Aldo...,"

"I knew I shouldn't have said anything to you, you're no help at all."

A few weeks later Aldo asked Rosie if she'd like to go to the pictures with him, but they had to take Ces along, her Dad said so. She was beside herself with excitement. He didn't have a girlfriend after all.

Cesare buttoned the cuffs on his crisp white shirt and drew the comb through his slicked-back raven hair. It was the first time he was going out on his own as a young man, he was pleased with the image in the mirror. He had to escort his sister on her date, but going off in Aldo's shiny new EF Holden was a treat. After they got home from the pictures, Cesare felt quite grown up. He considered his future as a man, although he didn't have any idea of what to expect.

He had a staggered start to employment over a year ago when the boss at the Wool Stores discovered he was underage and sent him back to school. Six months later he'd returned to work there for a while, but now he had a new job at the Woollen Mills which was much better work and paid more money. Now he, Rosie and Sil all worked at the mill. They each had a different role in the process of raw wool being treated to produce blankets and other woollen products. The vast factory floor hummed and clunked with machinery and employees performing their various tasks. The finishing siren wailed for the end of the afternoon shift, and the girls left through the exit door.

"Come on Rosie, please." Silvana jabbed her sister in the ribs, a pleading look in her eyes. "Just this once, please."

"Just this once, we've been past there so many times now it's shameful."

"Oh, come on sis."

"All right," she sighed. "But we have to hurry because I don't want Aldo waiting for us again like he had to last time." Rosie couldn't help but chuckle to herself at her sister's pleasure. They headed down the hill to go past the building where Alberto D'Alesio was painting. He'd seen these girls several times now as they walked by; initially, Alberto was unaware that 'he' was the object of the younger sister's admiration. Now they were waving to each other and Silvana would cough or laugh out loud to catch his attention.

Alberto had recently come from Pettorana in the Abruzzo region. He arrived in September 1960 after a three week trip on the ship *'Roma'.* Alberto was 21 and didn't want to join the army for the compulsory term expected of all young Italian men. He could've gone to Venezuela to join his brother where they earned good money polishing concrete floors. But he decided to come to Australia and was sponsored by his sister's husband, Peter Andreotti. Giuseppina had come to Albany six years earlier and was recently married to Peter. Albert lived with his uncle and aunt on their farming property in Narrikup. He got a painting job in Albany because he had experience. When his apprenticeship in Italy as a mechanic couldn't be completed, he started painting with his brother-in-law in Pettorana and then went to work as a painter at the hospital in Sulmona, near his village home.

A young English girl arrived in Fremantle on Thursday with her large family. The *'Arcadia'* had a dubious history. When they were due to sail away from the shores of England and the anchor was lowered to hold the ship fast, a strong wind caused the anchor to rip a massive hole in its bow. They had to wait for it to be repaired before their journey to Australia could continue. It sailed across the ocean without any other major incident. Her parents and older brother had paid their ten pounds to emigrate, but she and the other children had free passage.

At 15, Patricia Ann was already a mature young woman, and she hoped this change would be a positive experience in her life. They were processed through Customs and then collected by her aunt and uncle who were their sponsors. 'Welcome to Australia, the land of milk and honey', she thought. They were all crammed into the same state house together, she and her six siblings and parents with their relatives. Monday morning arrived, and Patricia Ann was taken to the Albany Woollen Mills to start training for a job arranged for her by her aunt. Silvana Nostrini had to show her how to use the machine she would learn to operate. They became good friends in a short time.

One morning at tea break, Pat said she had to work overtime today. Sil couldn't wait any longer and took a cutting from a magazine out of her pocket and slid it across to Pat. She indicated with her eyes not to show anyone else in the lunch room. Pat took a look and smiled. When they were back at their machine, they giggled behind their hands at their mischief. The spinning machine whirred loudly as the wool strands from a large bobbin stretched thick thread over the roller. When the fibre was spun fine, it wound onto a smaller cotton-reel bobbin and was then woven into fabric for tweed suits and police shirts. No-one could hear the girls' private discussion over the factory floor noise.

"Shall we get some?"

"Do you think it'll work?" Pat yelled back into her friend's ear.

"I do, at least I hope so." Sil laughed as she pushed the filament with a rod into place. "But where shall we get it sent? My Mum wouldn't be happy about it."

"Use the address at my Aunty's place."

"Okay, I'll fill out the form tonight, and we can post it tomorrow." The girls paid attention to their work before they got told off for talking but now and then they gave each other a sly glance and smiled. A week later a jar of Sabrina cream for flat-chested girls arrived in the mail addressed to Patricia, but her aunty caught them out and roasted them for even considering such nonsense.

"Now we'll never know if it would've worked or not," Sil was disappointed.

"Yeah, and what a waste of money that was. Oh well, at least we tried." Then they got the giggles and laughed until they cried at their silliness. Pat's fresh start in this new country wasn't without its difficulties, but it was about to get better.

"Hey, Pat, my brother wants to go on a date with you," Sil probed her friend for a reaction.

"Really? He doesn't even know me."

"But he likes what he sees, and asked me to make arrangements for him. You can come with Albert and me to the pictures. Cesare will be there too because he has to come with us anyway. My Dad's fussy about that."

"I suppose it would be all right then. You can pick me up from the tyre shop on the corner near where I live." Pat explained where the tyre shop was and drew a mud map on a scrap of paper for her to show Albert. "What time should I be there?"

"Is 6.30pm okay for you? Albert has a black car now. He has a Lambretta scooter, but every time I get on it, the stupid thing won't go. When we go to the beach, Rosie has to go on Albert's scooter, and I have to go with Cesare on his Vesper. It's embarrassing, and I don't get to put my arms around Albert, I have to hold onto my brother instead."

"That bike is fickle, don't worry about it. Besides, you can sit right next to Albert in the car. I'll see you then." No-one was concerned about where she might be or who she might be with, so Pat didn't have to worry about that. And there was no way she was going to tell them they lived in a condemned house down the road from the tyre shop. It had become uncomfortable living with aunty, and Pat's family had shifted a couple of weeks ago. Her Dad didn't even know they'd moved yet, he was off at his job with a railway gang working out in the bush somewhere.

The black EK Holden pulled up at the kerb, Silvana wound down the front passenger window and called out.

"Hop in, Pat. We want to get good seats at the pictures, you know, in the back row." Pat opened the door and climbed in. Cesare nodded.

"Hello," he said.

"Hello," she replied. Sil prattled on about what they'd done during the afternoon.

The back row was full by the time they got there, but it didn't matter, and they never got to sit there anyway, others always filled those seats first. Pat enjoyed the company of her new friends. After the pictures, they all got back in the car to drop her off at the tyre place again. She would walk down the road in the dark because it wasn't too far. As she opened the door, Cesare spoke again for the second time in the whole evening.

"Good night."

"Good night," Pat replied. And that was, apparently, their first date. Cesare enjoyed it so much he asked Sil to arrange another date for the next weekend. They went down to Middleton Beach with Albert and Sil who wandered off in front of them along the shore, holding hands. Cesare and Pat followed them, and when the others stopped after a bit for a kiss and cuddle, Cesare took the cue and kissed Pat too, and that was it. Love bloomed.

Aldo approached Jack while he worked in the shed out the back. He had serious business to discuss.

"Jack, can I have a minute? I know you're busy, but I want to talk to you about Rosie." Jack immediately stopped what he was doing and looked directly at Aldo.

"Mah..., and what do you want to say?" Aldo swallowed hard and broached the subject that constantly consumed his thoughts.

"I want to marry her, Jack. I've waited for her to grow up and I'm sure she loves me. I'd like your permission to ask her if she'll marry me." Silence sat between them.

"Do you love her, Aldo?"

"Absolutely, I do."

"Where will you live?"

"We could turn the storeroom here into a cottage, if you'd be happy about that."

"Yes, that's a good idea. It would only be small though."

"That doesn't matter. We can save up enough money to build our own house in time."

"Mah..., well, I have my concerns about your age difference. Fourteen years is a huge gap, Aldo. What about when you get older? She might want to go and do things you probably won't want to do. Have you thought about that?"

"I've thought about a lot of things. And I knew you'd worry about the age difference, but the truth is, Jack, I don't think it will be a problem. If it becomes an issue in the future, we'll deal with it when the time comes. I'm sure you'd agree we are both capable of doing that."

"I don't deny you that young man. Our Rosie is quite the grown up at the tender age of 17. Let me talk to Emily about this before I give you my answer, can you wait for me to do that?"

"I've waited this long, what's another day or two?"

Aldo smiled and walked away with his hands pushed into his trouser pockets, and he whistled cheerfully as he went. Jack watched him from the shed door and shook his head. He remembered what it was like, to have to wait such a long time, but his daughter was so young.

At bedtime, Jack and Emily lay in bed talking it through, discussing the good things and not so good things about the situation.

"You do realise, husband dear, she is the same age as I was when we wanted to get married, but the war interfered with our plans."

"Mah..., but don't forget there's only three years difference between us two."

"True and yet Rosie has confided in me Aldo is the man for her. She doesn't want a silly teenager, and she wants to marry someone sensible and caring and Italian. He is that, and more. I can see they love each other and I don't have a problem with it. I'd be pleased to have Aldo as part of our family, officially, I mean, because he is already anyway."

"I'm probably just being the overprotective father who's not willing to let his daughter go."

"What do you mean by *'probably'*, I'd say you definitely are," Emily rolled towards Jack and kissed him. That was the end of the conversation, and they cuddled up together without another thought of an impending wedding. Jack realised it was a good thing for them all. He let Aldo know they had their blessing.

Aldo worked on the weekends because he needed the extra income to get married. He was an expert bricklayer and got the best results building chimneys, fireplaces and hearths for wood stoves. Chimneys had to be constructed to draw properly, and he had plenty of practice building dozens of them for Polish and German immigrants in town. Jack and Aldo set to work fitting out the cottage each evening after dinner. They lined the walls, put a ceiling in and built cupboards for a kitchenette. It needed painting and then it would be ready for furniture. The tiny cottage would be a welcoming home for the couple after their honeymoon.

Albany Bridal Dress Shop was opposite Foy's Department Store on the corner of Aberdeen and York Streets. An eager Rosie and Emily walked in through the open front door and admired the silk, satin and lace wedding dresses. The shop assistant helped Rosie put on a beautiful gown with a lace and ribbon panel down the front of the full skirt, and the bodice had a scalloped neckline and short sleeves. Sheer lace trimmed opera length fingerless gloves that matched the dress, and a lace-trimmed short veil on a circle of flowers completed the bridal outfit.

"What do you think, Mum?" Rosie smiled at her mother. "Do you like this on me?"

"I do, Rosie, you look beautiful," Emily croaked with emotion at the sight of her daughter dressed as a bride.

This was it, the right gown for her wedding. Rosie also fell in love with a pink quilted dressing gown, and mother and daughter decided it should be included in her trousseau. All the items were put on lay-by and had to be paid off before Christmas. Rosie took the gown off and put her polka dot dress and pink stiletto's back on. She smiled at the thought of when she and Aldo had gone window shopping after the pictures one Saturday evening and discussed the engagement rings in White's jewellery shop in York Street.

Aldo had gone back and bought the white gold one she loved best and gave it to her as a surprise. 'I've got something for you,' he'd said and handed her the box. Then he added, as he put the ring on her finger, that it had cost him plenty. Of course, she said yes when he asked her to marry him. They set the wedding date for New Year's Eve, two weeks before her eighteenth birthday.

The last day of December arrived, and the bride was dressed. Her bridesmaid looked elegant in her knee-length short-sleeved frock and, Nadia was the flower girl in her lacy dress, white shoes and socks and circle of flowers in her hair. The whole family looked handsome in their finery for the occasion. The father-of-the-bride had tears in his eyes as he walked his eldest daughter down the aisle of St Joseph's Catholic Church to meet Aldo waiting for her at the altar.

'Was it so long ago since she came into the world?' Giovanni thought. She almost didn't make it then, and now here she was, getting married. Jack's emotions almost bubbled over but the radiant look on Rosie's face quelled his fears, and he stood resolute as the priest asked the question.

"Who gives this woman to be married to this man?"

"I do," Jack responded and took his seat. The formalities were taken care of, and then the celebration dinner was enjoyed by family and friends. The Master of Ceremonies announced the father-of-the-bride would give his speech.

"Today my daughter Rosanna has become a married woman. Emily and I are pleased to welcome Aldo as a son-in-law into our family. Eight years ago Rosie arrived in Australia, a little girl with a determination to succeed in her life wherever it led. At a young age, she was already mature and had a great sense of responsibility. We know Aldo recognised our Rosie as a steady and capable girl and was prepared to wait for her. The day has finally come, Aldo, and we appreciate your patience. You may need more of it in the future as a husband to our daughter who has a mind of her own. At least I won't have you both taking turns to ask if you can go out for an extra night of the week anymore. But really, we hope you both enjoy your lives together as husband and wife and may all your troubles be little ones."

A chuckle ran through the seated guests, and they charged their glasses for the toast.

"To the bride and groom," Jack raised his glass, and an echo of voices repeated his words. The cake was cut, and they danced the bridal waltz before the handsome couple left for their honeymoon together. Emily cried on Jack's shoulder as the newlyweds drove away with cans rattling along the road behind them bearing a hand-painted *'Just Married'* sign.

"It's all right, love, she'll be back in a few days time."

"I know, she was a beautiful bride, wasn't she?" Emily sniffed and got her hankie out of her handbag.

"Yes, she was, and I looked around tonight while everyone was enjoying themselves, and I must say it pleased me to see our healthy, happy and prosperous family together. We've almost made the distance in this journey of ours for a better life. I'm happy, very happy." Jack squeezed her to his side and pecked a kiss on the top of her head.

Cesare pulled up on his Vesper to collect his girlfriend from the state house that had finally been allocated to Pat's family. Pat had heard the bike and went down the front steps to meet him. She was so slim and pretty, her curly hair was a bit unruly, but she combed it back to keep it under control. Ces looked up to see her wearing the deep rich red silk cheongsam dress she'd bought in Singapore on the way to Australia. It was stunning, and he loved her to wear it, but it was a problem with the Vesper because she had to sit sideways. Pat didn't mind because it meant she had to hang on tighter, so she didn't slide off the seat. They rode into town, parked in York Street and sat at a table in the Wildflower Cafe while they waited for their order. At least Ces was more talkative these days.

"Cesare, I've booked in to do night school."

"Really, what're you going to do?"

"Typing and shorthand classes, so I can get a secretarial job one day."

"That's good, but how are you going to get there? And do you think you'll cope with working all day and doing that as well?"

"It won't be easy, and I expect I'll get homework. I'll have to walk to the high school after work and then walk home afterwards. It's twice a week, but I want to do it."

"Maybe I can pick you up occasionally. I hope it's not going to be too much for you."

"I'm sure I can manage it. It's my dream, and I want to give it a go."

Cesare was secretly proud of his Patricia Ann, she was an intelligent girl, and he admired her ambition. After their date they kissed and cuddled in a dim corner of the verandah for quite a while, not wanting to leave each other. The flyscreen door opened and banged shut; Pat's father emptied the teapot over the side of the verandah railing and stomped back inside.

"I think that's Dad's hint it's time for you to go home, Ces."

"Just as well we weren't standing at the bottom of the steps, hey, otherwise I would have copped cold tea all over me," he chuckled and thought he'd better remember that just in case it happened again.

CHAPTER TWENTY-TWO

Monumental Decisions

Bruno's sawmill had been packed up, and Jack went to work for Peter Rizzi at Denbarker. Jack ran the large milling business and kept the men busy, made sure the orders were filled and checked transport arrangements were organised to deliver goods on time. Peter bought the Menegola mill in Albany, and Jack was finally able to work closer to home. He didn't have to leave quite so early in the morning and usually got home at a much more civil hour in the evening.

Clearing the farmland at Narrikup continued on weekends, and now Jack had a bit more available income, he paid for someone to bulldoze the trees and scrub in the next section. Burning off the windrows still needed to be done, and he had to prepare the soil to plant grain for haymaking before the next inspection. It would be quicker with the advantage of mechanical help this time. The tree trunks cleared previously on the property had been sawn into stumps, bearers and joists for the floor and Jack had started to build the house. Posts for the framework were up, and the roof rafters were the final stage to be done. Cesare and Pat would go out to pick rocks, fence a section and spread super on Saturday or Sunday to help develop the farm. One weekend they sat on the steps to eat their lunch and enjoy a sunny break.

"Snake!" Cesare yelled. Pat immediately jumped up from the step and vaulted onto the water tank platform to get as far away as possible from the reptile. She'd never seen a snake before, and she watched, terrified, as the tiger snake slithered across in front of them. Ces killed it and placed his trophy over the handlebars of the scooter to take home and show his Mum. When cars passed them on the road drivers would toot, and passengers pointed at the snake in horror. Emily was not impressed either.

Aldo had acquired Narrikup land in Jackson Road from a French developer, Mr L'Afanute. After months of grubbing out acres of tree suckers with the back of an axe and picking roots, the owner didn't have sufficient money to pay for the work he'd done but had given a portion of the title to him instead of payment. Aldo wanted to plough and seed 100 acres of the land, but he had to borrow money to do it.

When he applied for a loan from the Commonwealth Bank, he realised he didn't have the title deed because Mr L'Afanute still had it in his office drawer. Once that was collected, Aldo arranged the loan and asked Rino Cavazzi, from his home village in Italy, to fence the perimeter of his land for him. He and Rosie built a house and lived there after years of living in the tiny cottage in Elphinstone Road.

The mill on Albany Highway had been bought out by the timber milling company, Millar's, and after a time Jack left to lay blocks and bricks with Aldo for George Hodgson. This job was the best he'd had so far, and Jack was home on time for dinner each evening with his family. They'd finish their meal and clean up. Jack would carry the lantern and Emily would take the cups of coffee into the lounge room. It had a ceiling now and a couple of easy chairs with a small homemade table between them.

"Emily, I found out today George won the subcontract from the monumental stonemason, Howard Hartman, to rebuild that Anzac Memorial on Mt Clarence they've been talking about, and he's asked me to be in charge of the project," Jack sounded pleased with the chance to stretch his abilities.

"That'll be a challenge for you. Where did it come from again?" Emily knew it was in the Middle East somewhere.

"Port Said."

"Oh, we went past there on the ship, but I don't remember much about it, probably because I was sick."

"The monument got damaged during that Suez conflict in 1956. Apparently, a mob of angry Egyptians smashed up the statue in just a few hours, and there are some bullet holes in the granite blocks. They have to be put back together the same way as the original structure. Every block has a number because they're made to fit into each other, and can't just go anywhere. When all the trouble settled down the Arabs gave Australia permission to move it. They're recasting another statue to replace the one that had been there since 1932. It's being made by the Battaglia Brothers, from Milan. So, how about that?"

"Interesting."

"Mah..., did we get any mail today?"

"Oh yes, I forgot to tell you a letter arrived from Nino. He asked if we're going to come back to live in Italy again. Why do they keep doing that? They know we're staying here, we've already become naturalised Australians and now Rosie's pregnant I won't be going anywhere."

"I suspect they miss you more since your Papa passed away and that's why they keep asking." A small sigh escaped Emily's lips at his comment. "You're happy now though, aren't you, love?"

"Life has its ups and downs wherever you live." Jack turned his face toward his wife to see her expression and check she was okay. Emily smiled at him.

"Remember the time when Geoff Preston turned up with a washing machine he made from spare parts for me. He said he was tired of seeing me slave over the copper and wringing sheets out by hand, that was a happy day. I wouldn't have got one of those in Italy, even now. Geoff didn't know we washed everything by hand in the fountain at home."

"No, I'm sure he didn't. He's a good man."

"You're right, he is, and Olive is a lovely friend. When you go to Tognetti's shop tomorrow to collect the bread, can you get some parmesan cheese, polenta and some more mortadella? Say hello to Franca for me when you see her, I can't get into town until later in the week, but I'll catch up with her then."

"Sure, I'll tell her."

Jack and his team laid the foundations for the Desert Mounted Corps Memorial. He directed a crane to lift the numbered blocks into place, and the joints were pointed up with mortar. Jack built internal walls within the block work, and the cavity was filled with concrete. As the base grew, a scaffold was erected around the walls, and the labourers used a ladder to bring buckets of mud up for Jack. Cesare often went to work and helped his Dad at the site on the weekend.

'Australia and New Zealand 1916 – 1918' is inscribed on the granite in block letters, and a bronze plaque is in the centre of the base. A semi-circular wall wraps around the sides and rear of the massive pillar and granite paving slabs cut by Howard Hartman from his Mt Melville quarry complete the setting. The wooden crate with the bronze statue was dismantled, only to discover one of the horses had been damaged on the voyage to Australia. It had to be sent back to Europe for repairs because no one in Australia had the skills to fix it. Eventually, it was returned and craned into position, the sculpture of the Australian and New Zealand soldiers and their horses was placed in its lofty home. The views of King George Sound and Princess Royal Harbour are magnificent, and Emu Point and Middleton Beach stretch out beyond the natural grey-green frame of native scrub on Mt Clarence.

Prime Minister Robert Menzies unveiled the tribute on October 11, 1964. Every year on April 25 a dawn service is held at the monument. This significant date is dedicated to the Australian and New Zealand Forces in recognition of the soldiers who fought in World War I. For many, it was the last glimpse of Australia as they sailed away from their homeland. The same date in 1945 was important for Italians to commemorate Liberation Day from Fascism and the celebrated anniversary of the resistance. As a new Australian, Jack was pleased to be a part of the project and his family were proud of him.

Albert plucked up the courage to ask for Sil's hand in marriage when he and Jack had gone to collect material from Elphinstone Road. Jack was building a house for Albert's brother-in-law, and he was helping out. Albert and Sil became engaged and prepared to be married on May 15, 1965. Sil borrowed her future sister-in-law's long-sleeved traditional wedding dress that had been made in Italy, she had a tiara for her veil and Nadia was a flower girl for her sister. Aldo and Rosie had their first son, Jack and Emily's first grandchild by then.

The Albany Italian Club community raised finance to build a clubhouse. The members worked together and used their many skills to construct the building. Jack built brick walls, erected the roof and put timber flooring down. There were plenty of labourers to help out. People from all provinces in Italy came together to participate in shared cultural activities. Emily was on the ladies committee and helped organise annual events like pasta and tomato sauce making. The men played bocce and arranged the sausage making day at the beginning of winter.

Jack sat at the table after dinner with the newspaper spread out in front of him. He was nodding off to sleep.

"Come on, Jack, go and have a shower or we'll be late."

"Huh. What for?"

"The dance, at the Club tonight, the kids are ready, and I'm going to get changed now."

Dances were held nearly every weekend, and Italian songs were sung just like they used to at home. They enjoyed being together and sharing these traditions with a few Spanish, Polish and Australian friends.

It was raining on the way into town, and Jack had been quietly thoughtful before he posed an odd question.

"Emily, have you got an old white sheet I can have?"

"There's one with a hole in the corner of it that I was going to mend. What do you want it for?"

"The Roman Night in a few weeks time, I want to wear a toga! I'll make a wreath to wear on my head and a medallion on a gold chain, too. Everyone can say 'Hail Caesar' to me, and it'll be fun." He smiled. "What are you going to wear?"

"I thought I'd get some light blue soft and flowy material for a long dress. I might add a silver belt and headband or something like that. I'll go to Wilf's Fabrics and see what I can find cheap. Maybe you could have a red cape or sash as well, shall I have a look?"

"Yes, that sounds perfect."

"Did you know the Moronis are having pre-dinner drinks at their place? They've invited us and a few others to join them."

"Good, maybe we can take some photos with everyone dressed up."

On other occasions, they wore traditional dress and danced the tarantella.

The children participated, and when they were exhausted, they'd go to sleep on a blanket on the floor or in the car before they were taken home to bed. At the annual Christmas Tree function, Jack was always Father Christmas dressed in the red and white suit with a pillow tucked up in the front of the jacket, a white beard, floppy red hat and an affected deep voice to emulate Santa.

Ces drove Pat home in his Dad's van after a Saturday night dance at the Italian Club.

"When we get married, we can go and live in the house at Narrikup," Cesare said to Pat while they chatted before it was time for her to turn in.

"So we are getting married, are we?" Pat looked straight at him.

"Yes, you want to get married, don't you?"

"Yes, if that's a proposal."

"Dad and I have been talking, and we think it would be a good idea for us to move out there. Mum doesn't want to leave town anyway. What do you reckon?"

"It would be great, I'd like to do that."

Wedding plans were under way, they wanted to get married on Jack and Emily's wedding anniversary, but the venue was unavailable on that date. Saturday, October 22, 1966 was booked instead. Then there was the issue of Pat not being a Catholic, they could only marry at St Joseph's if she took lessons, which she did. Rosie was pleased when Pat asked to borrow her wedding dress, but she chose a different veil and headpiece to wear with it.

Pat visited her friend and future sister-in-law, Sil, who was pregnant with her first child. She and Albert had moved into the tiny cottage at home after their previous rental arrangement with Albert's uncle had fallen through. They had begun to build a house in Drew Street, and they'd put up a carport made from leftover scrap metal retrieved from the silo being built at the wharf. Cesare and Pat had planned to live in the cottage until the house in Narrikup was ready. Now an alternative was needed, and soon.

With Silvana's borrowed wedding ring on her left hand, Pat faced the State Housing Commission interview with paperwork in hand, pleading for a home they needed desperately, she'd said. So now they had to wait for the red tape to be processed. A week before the wedding they received advice they had a two bedroom home available for them. Pat was pleased, and it was just in the nick of time too. The wedding went off without a hitch, and the bride and groom settled into their own home – despite the 'You'll be sorry, it'll never work!' comment from her aunt.

A telegram arrived from Italy, delivered by the postman who stood at the front door. Emily wiped her hands on the apron she wore and said a shaky 'thank you'. It wasn't usually good news when you got a telegram. She took a deep breath and reached for a knife out of the drawer to open the envelope. Tears streamed down her face; Mama was gone. One of the blood transfusions she'd received for her anaemia was infected with hepatitis and Rosa had become seriously ill and died. *'I won't ever get to see you again, Mama'*. Emily knew her Mama was heartsore as well, with two of her daughters living so far away from home, it had caused her to be depressed along with her other ailments.

Farming to make a living at Narrikup would require more land because the cows had only just enough feed in the summer as it was. Jack wanted to buy the block that sat between his place and Bruno's which would give him enough land to allow the farm to make a viable living. He had a handshake agreement with the owner and paperwork was put in place at the bank to borrow the money to buy it. Jack was pleased with the prospect because the beef market prices were high.

A couple of weeks later with a bank cheque in hand, Jack drove to the neighbouring property to seal the deal. A stranger came across the paddock to meet him.

"Hello, how can I help you?" the man asked.

"I've come to see the owner, I have a cheque to buy this place," Jack smiled.

"That's interesting, sir, you see I am the owner. I just bought this land myself." Confused, Jack shook his head and looked about for the man he knew to be the owner.

"No, that's not right. I'm buying it, I had an agreement made already. I've been to the bank and here's the money, right here. Where is he?"

"I already told you, I own this place now. I'll go and get the title deed to prove it if you don't believe me. Just wait a tick."

Shock seeped into Jack's bones. He was wrong, *'this was going to be my land'*. Who did this bloke think he was anyway? It can't be right, surely not.

"Here you go, there it is. See it says right here – there's my name, this is the property title number, and it's all legal and above board. It's true just like I told you." The man wasn't unkind but held the documents and his driver's licence to prove who he was. The papers had the original owner's correct name and signature, it was right. Jack paled, he'd been duped to believe they had a concrete arrangement, but he'd had the dirty done on him. Shoulders slumped, Jack walked back to the car and drove home to tell Emily.

The grappa bottle hit the table with a thud, and Jack's demeanour wasn't one to be broached. The coffee percolated on the stove, and Emily poured the black liquid into the tiny Italian cups. He tipped a generous amount of the alcohol into his coffee and stirred it. He felt like pouring a full glass of the stuff, but that wasn't his way. He'd deal with his anger, and not by getting drunk, although the idea had appealed to him on his way home from the farm. He'd have to rethink his plans for the future. Maybe he would build his beautiful wife a new house because she certainly deserved it. He watched her sip her coffee, not saying a word, she gave him the time he needed to work through his emotions. Jack smiled, yes, that's what he'd do. He loved her more than ever.

"I can't believe it, Dad's sold the farm," a distraught Cesare told his wife.

"What?" Pat thought he must have it wrong.

"It's true, and we have to go and help Dad collect all our stuff on the weekend."

"I don't believe it." Pat shook her head, tears stinging her eyes.

Jack was approached by another neighbour who offered to buy his block when he heard it was going to be sold. Documents were signed, and money had been transferred with the title deed handed over. The equipment and other possessions had to be transported to Elphinstone Road. Jack loaded up the two cows he had left, Ces drove the tractor back, and Pat took the car with the super-spreader tied down with ropes on the trailer. She hadn't towed anything before and was scared stiff, Pat's knuckles were white as she gripped the steering wheel and concentrated on the road ahead, nervous as a kitten, but made it home in one piece. It was a sad end to a multitude of dreams for them.

Part Three
Ever After

CHAPTER TWENTY-THREE

Return Tickets

THE SUITCASES WERE WEIGHED IN, tagged and taken to be loaded onto the aircraft. Emily stood behind Jack in the queue as they went through security at Perth International Airport. How very different it was to their previous voyage across the globe.

"Do you have our passports ready?"

"Yes, they're tucked into the side pocket of my handbag with our boarding passes."

"How are you feeling?"

"I'm a bit nervous but I know everything will be all right, and you're here. I can't believe we're doing this, going home, but Italy's not our home anymore..., and I don't want to stay there either, at least that's what I think at the moment. I am looking forward to seeing everyone in Morbegno. I wonder if it's changed, probably not much."

"No, I doubt it's changed at all."

The boarding call finally came, and Jack held Emily's hand to help calm her nerves as they walked through the aerobridge to the plane. He smiled at her.

"This is a bit better than a steep and slippery gangplank buffeted by the wind."

A smartly dressed air hostess directed the passengers to the correct aisle for their seats. Jack's was next to a window, and Emily's seat was on the aisle. The crew helped place their hand luggage in the overhead locker, and they adjusted their seatbelts. Jack was excited by the adventure of flying, but Emily wasn't so sure about it.

"At least I can't get seasick, and I hope I won't need that." She pointed to the brown sick-bag stuffed into the pocket of the chair in front of her. Jack looked out the window while they taxied to the runway. It was a dull day, a bit cloudy and there'd been a shower of rain. Everything was wet, and a weak shaft of sunlight broke through to reveal puddles with oil slick shining in bright colours. They were amazed that in 24 hours they would be in Italy at the height of summer.

Rome Airport was bustling with activity, Jack and Emily walked through long corridors and numbered gates to get to the domestic terminal where an Alitalia flight would take them to Malpensa Airport in Milan. Nino and Adriana were going to meet them there, so they wouldn't have to get a train. Not that it mattered to them because they'd been used to it in the past, but her brother and his wife couldn't wait to see them. They all had a lot of catching up to do, you could only write so much in letters, and international phone calls were expensive.

Nino was anxious. They stood at the main gate, eyes searching; hoping they would still recognise each other. People didn't change that much, surely, even though it had been 20 years. Then there they were, toting their suitcases and looking as handsome as ever. A tearful reunion opened the floodgates to incessant chatter all the way back to the village.

Morbegno had changed little, they recognised familiar landmarks, buildings and people. Thankfully Jack's father, Cesare, was still alive and it was a joy to see him again, but a gaping hole was left with the absence of their other departed parents.

"Papa..." Jack embraced his father, the men silently clung to each other for a time. "Emilia," Cesare tenderly hugged his daughter-in-law. It was difficult to speak with the emotion that rose up from their hearts into their throats. A celebration with family squeezed in tightly around a long table shared sausage, polenta, a green salad and home-made red wine. A wooden board of Valtellina cheeses invited Jack to pick up a large wedge and pare off a slice. He passed it to Emily. She took it and savoured the flavour with her eyes closed. Jack ate some as well. That's something they'd missed, there wasn't cheese like that in Australia. Stories from before they left were retold, new adventures discussed and tears of emotion shed at the pain they'd endured during the changes in their lives.

A sweet summer breeze fluttered the lace curtain at the window, it caught Emily's eye, and she sat up in bed while Jack slept. The framed image of the Madonna was still in her place on the wall. Memories flooded her thoughts and a realisation of the woman she had become surprised her. Much more confident and independent than she ever expected herself to be, a sense of pride surged through her. It was worth it all to be this Emily. Jack stirred and looked up at his wife.

"You're awake early, love."

"I couldn't sleep any longer, but I didn't want to disturb you. Thank you, Jack."

"What for?"

"For loving me, for taking me on a journey in my ordinary life that I didn't even want to do."

"Mah..., been reminiscing have you?"

"I guess so, and I've just realised all we've been through has made us into the people we are today, and it's good. It's a very good way to be, and I don't have any regrets. Although, of course, if I knew back then it would be all right by now, maybe I might've reacted differently at the time."

"We never know what to expect in life, and just deal with what we have to when we have to."

"I've learned that, but I think I would've been a different person if I'd stayed here."

"Probably ..." Jack chuckled and reached for her.

Steve boarded his flight to Melbourne with the WA State Country Boys Hockey team. The group of young men had a two-hour wait at

Tullamarine Airport before flying to Hobart. Enamoured by the airport, jet plane and uniformed crew, this was his first flight at fifteen-years-old. He was excited by the whole adventure. He'd only been as far as Perth before.

The team consisted of young men from Albany, Geraldton, Narrogin and Bunbury who'd been selected from trials after the High Schools' Country Week sporting competition. They'd only played together as a team a few times but their skill sets blended well, and they were a force to be reckoned with. The tour included playing games in Launceston, Devonport and Bernie and after a successful journey, they returned home tired but ecstatic from the whole experience.

Going back to school was unsettling for Steve, he felt the 4th Year High School studies he was ploughing through weren't going to help him in his future. He didn't want an academic career. He decided to talk to his brother-in-law about a bricklaying apprenticeship. He liked to be outside, and he was strong and hard working. His dream of farming had been dashed when his Dad sold the property at Narrikup.

Aldo was surprised at Steve's request, and because Emily and Jack were in Italy, he didn't want to decide without their consent.

"But Aldo, I don't want to go to school anymore. I need a job," Steve insisted.

"Well, can you at least wait until Sunday and talk to your Mum and Dad when they ring at four o'clock?"

"I suppose so, I promise to work hard for you, and you can teach me everything you know."

"I'm sure you will, but it's the right thing to talk to your parents first. I have to find out about apprenticeship arrangements and requirements before you can start anyway."

The phone discussion was short, but they agreed to the opportunity. Steve stopped going to school and started work with Aldo straight away. The school office found out eventually when they pursued him for truancy not long after Jack and Emily returned from Italy.

Steve learned the trade well and attended Perth Technical School once a year for two weeks to study theory. It was a five-year apprenticeship, and even though the wages weren't high, he enjoyed his job. His Mum banked some money for him every week, and he saved up for a car of his own after he got his licence. A Morris Minor was all he could afford, but it meant he enjoyed the freedom of independence.

A letter arrived from Italy from Giuliana with good news. Emily's sister and family were coming to Australia! How exciting, it was going to happen sooner than she thought. When they were in Italy, much discussion about them emigrating had taken place around the meal table. Jack discovered Australia would only accept applications from people who had specific skills. Guido had done some rock wall building when he was younger, and Jack could sponsor him on that basis. Giuliana and her family could be close by because Albert and Sil had moved into their new home and the cottage was empty. Emily gave it a spring clean, made up beds and filled the pantry and fridge with food. It was her family coming here to live, and she didn't want them to face the dilemma's she'd had to when she first arrived.

Assistance from the Australian Government helped cover the cost of airfares, and Qantas tickets had been collected for two adults and two children. The flight left Rome and went via Melbourne. Giuliana had sent a telegram to let them know when they would arrive in Perth but it wasn't delivered until the morning they flew in from the Eastern States. An urgent phone call to friends in the city was made to arrange the collection of their relatives at the airport. Emily was disappointed they wouldn't make it in time to wait for them when they walked through the doors after going through Customs. She didn't want to let them down, but they couldn't get there in time.

"Can you see them?" Giuliana searched the faces in the crowd to see someone she knew.

"No, not yet, I can't. Oh no, he's sick again Giuliana. Quick, fix him up." Their three-year-old son had been airsick all the way from Melbourne and hadn't recovered after he got off the plane.

"There's our name on that sign." The Immigration Department took the family aside to an interview room with a stack of forms to be completed. Fortunately, Mrs Barbetti arrived in time to translate, and she took on the responsibility for shepherding the four Italians she'd never met before. They were signed over to her while Jack and Emily were on their way to the city.

"*Grazie, mille grazie, Senora,*" Giuliana was grateful for her help. The foreign family were well cared for while they waited for her sister and brother-in-law to come. Emily was anxious to get there, and they arrived late in the afternoon. A warm welcome dinner was enjoyed with the Barbetti's in their Perth suburban home, and after a good night's sleep, they all headed south.

"How much further do we have to go?" Guido asked Jack.

"A long way yet, I'm afraid. Distance is something you get used to in Australia." Jack smiled, he'd forgotten how far Perth to Albany seemed on his first trip back in 1950 nearly 23 years earlier.

"We're going to drive past the block in Narrikup so you can have a look on the way. It's been sold, but the new owner won't mind." After the already long drive, the four newcomers groaned inwardly.

"When are we going to get there?" the children asked their parents. They were tired and sore from sitting all day.

"Not long now," Jack said as he drove down York Street to show them the town before they headed to Elphinstone Road. They pointed out the Town Hall, Princess Royal Harbour and other points of interest along the way.

The Della Vedova family moved into the little cottage. Once they were settled, Guido got his Australian Driver's Licence and a job with Albany Industrial Services driving a truck for the owner, George Walmsley. Giuliana went to work at Borthwick's Abattoir and then took a position at the Albany Woollen Mills.

Bruno and Bruna Rizzi called in to see Jack and Emily on Sunday. The Della Vedova's joined them for a coffee. The afternoon stretched out as they discussed their plans.

"We're off to visit family in Italy for a couple of months. We want to know if you'd like to go and live out on the farm," Bruno addressed Guido and Giuliana. He offered them the chance to manage the property for him and share the profit because they intended moving to Perth on their return from Italy. Beef prices were high, and the income was sufficient to support both families.

"We'd love to do that, yes, we'll do it." Guido was pleased with the opportunity. The family of four packed up ready to move to Narrikup. George was disappointed to lose a good worker. He mentioned to Guido, when he handed in his notice, he didn't think the market would remain stable at that level. He let him know he could come back and work for him again if he wanted to in the future.

They enjoyed their time on the farm, but it wasn't a lasting arrangement. George's prediction proved correct, and the bottom fell out of the beef market. The Rizzi's were unable to follow through with their original plan. Giuliana and Guido borrowed money from the bank and bought the Albany Highway property Aldo had for sale. Guido returned to drive the truck during the week for Albany Industrial Services and built some rock retaining walls on the weekends at Albany Senior High School which provided them with extra income, and honoured his immigration sponsorship.

Jack and Emily flew to Argentina in 1974 to visit Anna-Maria and her family in Buenos Aires and then planned to go on to Italy and Switzerland to see Jack's sister, Maria and her husband, Ugo. After a sad farewell to Anna-Maria and Antonio, they boarded their flight to Italy.

"Jack, I'm surprised and disappointed at how my sister's family have to live. I didn't like to say anything while we were there in case someone heard me." Anna-Maria and her family lived in a concrete high rise apartment building with no space to spare, wages were low, and the cost of inner-city living was high and entirely different from their country lifestyle.

"I know what you mean. Antonio can't even afford to use the car except for the occasional Sunday drive because the fuel is too expensive. And meat prices are outrageous! You'd think with exporting top quality beef around the world that Argentines would get it cheaper."

"It makes me appreciate living in Australia. We are so much better off." Emily's face brightened, "Maybe they could come to Australia too! What do you think, Jack?"

Nadia got a job at the Zenith laundry, it was hot and hard work, but she didn't mind. She liked to fold the crisp white cotton sheets that spat out of the roller, but sorting personal laundry was her pet hate. She usually ended up doing the ironing because she was good at it and quite liked ironing, especially men's shirts. She wondered if the other girls deliberately didn't do a good job so they wouldn't get lumbered with it.

"Steve, I've got a friend at work who's a nice girl but she doesn't know many people, and I thought maybe you could take her out on a date." Nadia looked at her brother who was non-committal to her matchmaking. "I told her you would."

"You didn't even check with me first, that's nice Nard."

"Well you don't go out, and you haven't had a girlfriend yet, I thought I'd try and help."

"Okay, I suppose I'll have to now, won't I?" Nadia's cheeky grin stretched across her face.

"I 'spose so, I'll make the arrangements for Saturday night then, to go to the drive-in. You better keep some money to pay for the tickets before Mum goes to the bank."

The weekend arrived and Steve worked with his Dad on Saturday morning laying bricks for the new house in David Street. He played a late afternoon hockey game, then after a shower and bite to eat he dressed in the clothes his sister had chosen for him to wear on his date. He wasn't sure about the whole idea, but was committed to it and would go ahead. Nadia had been grilled for information about the girl. All she could tell him was that her workmate had come from South Australia and was living in Albany by herself.

Steve had recently upgraded his car for a second-hand orange Hillman Hustler. It was in good condition and more reliable with room in the boot for his tools. He drove to town, down York Street and into Aberdeen Street to find the address Nadia had given him. He parked the car and sat there for a few minutes. He took a deep breath or two. A girl with long fair hair wearing a blue top, jeans and brown leather toe-thongs on her feet came out of the front door. She didn't look like the friend Nadia had described, but she approached the car. Steve wound down the window.

"Hello, my name's Sheryl. And you're Steve?"

"Yes."

"I'm sorry, but my friend has decided she doesn't want to go out tonight."

"Oh, okay."

"But, look since you're here, you're welcome to come to the coffee house next door if you like. Our Baptist youth group runs an open house there. You can buy a cuppa and raisin toast; and we play pool, sit around the fire and talk or sing some songs."

"Oh, okay." He didn't say much, played a game or two of pool then left a little while later.

The next Saturday Steve turned up again, and then came to play badminton on Tuesday nights in the hall across the road. Not long afterwards he joined the youth group on Fridays and church on Sunday nights. Sheryl was aware Steve appeared to be interested in her. She wasn't sure about that, but he was consistent. On Tuesday night he plucked up the courage to ask Sheryl to come and watch him play hockey on Saturday. She was going to be at a friend's place, but if he would pick her up from there, she was happy to go.

"Steve's here," someone called out from the front door. Sheryl picked up her bag to leave.

"I'll come too, I play hockey." Her friend invited herself along.

Steve nodded it was okay with a half shrug of his shoulder. Then she pushed in to get into the front seat. Sheryl sat in the back, and a realisation dawned on her, she was jealous. Her friend barged in on what was supposed to be her outing. Up until that moment, she wasn't sure what she felt, but she sure did now. They watched the game as best they could from the car, it was pouring rain, and they couldn't see much. Steve came back soaking wet, carrying his hockey stick, shin pads still stuffed under his long socks and beaming. They'd won their game. When he took his mouthguard out, he winked at Sheryl. And that was it, she was smitten, and they started going out.

Nadia came home from work one day and asked if she could go out with some girls from the laundry on Sunday afternoon. Her parents agreed after asking pertinent questions. She omitted to tell them the plan was to hang out where all the young men parked their cars along York Street.

John and his mate, Steve Lenson completed a Yorkie, a drive up and down the length of the main street, when they noticed Nadia with her friends.

"Come on John, ask her out. If you don't, I will. Let me out here, and you go for it." Lenny pushed his quiet friend to say hello to Nadia. John pulled up at the kerb and wound down the passenger side window of his Sandman Holden panel van. His view of Nadia was immediately obliterated by one of the other girls who poked her head in the window.

"I want to talk to Nadia please," John stated. Nadia smiled and spoke to him, pleased because she'd had a crush on him for a long time. They lived near each other and caught the same school bus for years before they went to work. She'd ride her bike to his house on Saturdays to see his sisters. Her Mum didn't mind her visiting the girls, but the reason she went was to see if John was home. She hoped she would end up with him one day. He was tall with brown hair and blue eyes from his Dutch heritage, and those things appealed to her. He was kind and a smart young man, Nadia liked that about him.

John went to see her during the week at the laundry in his lunch break. He wanted to pick her up after work on Friday and take her home. Emily said that was okay, and John asked permission to take Nadia out. Jack approved, only after he checked him out first.

"Where are you going all dolled up like that?" Steve took in his sister's attire.

"I'm going out with John Knuiman." Her brother knew John from school and hockey.

"What! No, you're not, no way."

"Yes, I am. John asked me, and we're going to the drive-in. Dad said it was all right." Nadia was miffed by her brother's sceptical attitude. "You can answer the door when he comes to pick me up. Then you'll see." She lifted up a defiant chin and went to collect her shoulder bag. A few minutes later the doorbell rang. No-one else would answer the door, so Steve had to.

"It is you! Um, Nard, John's here." He shook his head and glanced over his shoulder as they walked down the front steps of their new house in David Street to his car. John opened the door for her and off they went. The brother and sister and their respective girlfriend and boyfriend often went out together, sometimes for a meal at a restaurant or to the beach or just for a drive somewhere.

Planning a wedding in winter in Albany was risky, it could rain or hail, or it might be fine weather. John had asked Nadia to marry him, she said yes, and they set a date for sooner rather than later. He had driven from Geraldton to Albany for regular weekend visits since his job transfer with Shell nearly two years earlier. The return trips were taking their toll. He was tired and afraid he might have an accident with the sun in his eyes driving north-west late on Sunday afternoons. He wasn't a good cook and often made himself sick, he needed his soul mate beside him.

Judy, Nadia's dressmaker, made a white crepe gown trimmed with guipure lace for her wedding dress, two blue bridesmaid and two floral flower girl dresses. Nadia looked radiant on her wedding day, Saturday, July 30, 1977. The weather was kind, and the bride and her father were driven to St Joseph's Church in town. The bridesmaids were her future sisters-in-law, and two of her nieces were flower girls. John, his best man and groomsman wore two-tone blue suits, ruffle-fronted shirts, mullet hairstyles and platform shoes. All very seventies! The young men waited at the altar for the bridal procession, the mass was announced, and Nadia and John were married. It was a grand family affair and an extravagant celebration, a reception their parents were pleased to give them.

Emily struggled with letting her youngest daughter go, especially since she was going to live north of Perth, over 466 miles away. John promised his mother-in-law he would bring her home for visits. After the honeymoon, John was surprised when they drove through Bullsbrook, and Nadia asked if they were nearly there yet. She had no idea of how far away Geraldton was from Albany, and they were only on the outskirts of the capital city. Four and a half hours later they pulled into the drive of their love nest. They were happy, and John was well fed and taken care of, but his bride was lonely.

"Mum, I want to marry Sheryl," Steve braved the subject with Emily.

"She's a good girl, Steve, that's nice."

"But Mum, we'll be married in the Baptist Church."

"I thought so. Do you realise there'll be people who won't understand why you'd do that? Some of our friends will probably be offended."

"Yes, I know, Mum, but it's the same God we worship, just not the same denomination. I love her, and I want to marry her. It doesn't matter what other people think about us not getting married at St Joseph's."

"You're right Steve, I know you're happy, and that's what counts more than anything."

Steve bound up the stairs of Campion House where Sheryl worked at the Public Works Department office. She looked up from her typewriter, puzzled, he never came into the office. Sometimes he'd pick her up from work downstairs, but that was rare.

"Is something wrong?"

"No, I want to show you something."

"Oh, what's that?"

"Come on, you'll see."

They went downstairs together and drove to Spencer Park. Steve pulled up on the roadside near an empty block of land with a for sale sign posted in the middle of it.

"What do you think?"

"About what?"

"The block of land. This one on the corner."

"It's fine, but what does it have to do with me?"

"Well, you have to like it too if we build a house on it."

"Us?"

"Yes, so what do you think?"

"Don't you think you should ask me something else first?"

He looked blank, a dawning of what he was missing lit his face.

"Oh, will you marry me?"

"Yes, and yes, I like the block!"

A bright sunny day dawned on February 11, 1978. It was the day Steve and Sheryl tied the knot at Albany Baptist Church in Aberdeen

Street. The handsome groom, best man and groomsman stood when the pastor announced the bride had arrived. The procession began with the bridesmaids, followed by the flower girl and pageboy walking down the aisle. The smiling bride swathed in white French lace with a long train entered the church on her father's arm. Emily smiled, and Jack squeezed her hand as the couple repeated their vows to each other. The bride noticed there were only three rows of pews at the front of the church with people in them on the groom's side. They were mostly his immediate family and his hockey friends.

The reception at Hillside Lodge overlooked Princess Royal Harbour and was a stunning venue, all the guests were present to enjoy the evening of celebration. The bride and groom changed into their going away outfits and kissed their family and friends goodbye. Steve's orange Torana XU1 was decorated with toilet paper, loaded up with confetti and *'Just Married'* was written in lipstick on the back window, they got in and drove away for their planned honeymoon.

"There goes the last one," Jack commented. Emily couldn't reply, she was choked up with emotion and just nodded. Jack placed his arm around her, and they went to say goodbye to their guests before going home. Nadia and John had come down south for the wedding, and John was best man for Steve in the bridal party. Emily relished her youngest daughter's presence over the weekend.

Not long afterwards, John's parents visited Geraldton and realised how homesick Nadia was. They insisted on taking her back to Albany for a few weeks, and later she returned to have their first baby in her home town. John made his wife's welfare his priority and resigned from his position with Shell. They returned to Albany to live.

A nagging desire to see Anna-Maria's situation improve prompted Jack and Emily to offer her the opportunity to come to Australia and investigate the possibility of changing their lives. A return ticket was sent to Argentina for her to visit Albany. The extended family put in a share of money to pay for it, and the sisters saw one other again. Anna-Maria was pleased to meet nieces and nephews she'd only seen in photographs before. She enjoyed tours of family homes, local scenery and a sightseeing trip to Perth. Emotional talks about coming to live in Albany were a daily event, but it was only a holiday. Anna-Maria couldn't see past leaving their established pattern of living. All too soon she was back on the plane to return to South America.

CHAPTER TWENTY-FOUR

Adversity

A HEAVILY PREGNANT NADIA COLLECTED John from the hospital after his physiotherapy session on his injured leg. A slab of marble had fallen on it at work, and damaged bone, muscle and skin and needed regular treatment to save his leg.

"John, I'm worried about Mum, she had a strange twitch in her eye and kept rubbing it when I was there after dropping the kids off at school. I think I should go back and check on her, just to put my mind at ease. She's had it for a couple of days. Rosie was there, and they were supposed to go out, but Mum wasn't well enough."

"Okay, but I won't come in. I'll just wait in the car for you, it's too hard to walk up the steps or the driveway."

"That's fine. I'll just pop in and see if she's okay."

Nadia entered through the flyscreen door at the back of the house into the sunroom, her Mum wasn't in the kitchen or the lounge. Confused, she called out several times before hearing a moan from the bedroom. Emily lay on the floor beside the bed, mumbling for help.

"Mum! What happened? Did you fall? Did you hit your head?" Nadia started to panic.

"I can't get up, help me, please Nard."

Nadia decided that was not the best plan. She awkwardly put her Mum on her side and called Rosie to ring for an ambulance, and then went down and told John what was going on. Dad was out, and she went back to sit with her mother until the ambulance arrived. It didn't take too long, the St John Ambulance Service was just down the road. The paramedics carefully lifted Emily onto the stretcher and wheeled her down to load her into the vehicle when Jack arrived.

"What's going on? What happened to Mum?" Confused and upset, he looked at Nadia for some answers.

"We don't know, Dad. Mum collapsed, and I'm not sure if she fell off the stepladder in her room or if something else is going on. It might have something to do with her eye that's been worrying her for days. No-one knows anything at the moment. We have to get her to the hospital." The paramedics drove out slowly, and Rosie pulled up in the driveway. Jack got into the car with her, and they followed the ambulance to the emergency department.

Jack wrung his hands together, he had paled and was visibly shaken. Rosie felt a leaden lump in the pit of her stomach. She parked the car and arm-in-arm they went into the hospital to find their wife and mother.

Emily was given a thorough check-up, x-rays were taken and blood samples had been sent off to pathology. She lost consciousness again and was now under observation in the intensive care unit. Jack sat on the chair beside the bed. Moisture dampened his cheeks while he watched his beloved in a hospital gown with tubes in her arms and nose, no wiser than before about what had happened. Rosie stood beside him, and a nurse came to let her know other family members were waiting outside the room. Only two visitors were allowed at a time. Rosie nodded in understanding because the lump in her throat wouldn't allow any sound out of her mouth.

A parade of shocked family members in pairs passed through the ward. Jack sat on a chair in the corridor while he waited. His sons and daughters were sympathetic and encouraged him not to worry. Of course, he was worried, and he was scared. Rosie took Jack home in the late afternoon to get something to eat and help him gather his thoughts. He kept nagging about the tests.

"We have to wait for the results, Dad," she explained.

"Mah..., why does it take so long?"

"There are processes they have to work through. We'll know as soon as they can tell us. Get some rest, you look exhausted. I'll come back in the morning to get some of Mum's things and pick you up again." He agreed, and Rosie went home to take care of her own family. No-one slept very well that night.

Nothing of any significance showed up in the test results. Conscious again, Emily complained of a headache and a sore neck, possibly from the impact of the fall when she collapsed. They gave her Panadol and a heat pack, and a physiotherapist prescribed exercises in the heated pool to help relieve the neck pain.

When Emily went into a coma, discussion between Albany doctors and specialists in Perth attempted to reach a diagnosis for Emily's condition. Frustrated and angry, the family confronted the medical team to make a decision to send her to Perth. It took another week before they arranged transport to Royal Perth Hospital for a CT scan which wasn't available in Albany. The Royal Flying Doctor Service flew to Albany and collected Emily from the airport to transport her to the city hospital. Results proved she had suffered a stroke caused by a ruptured brain aneurysm and the headache and neck pain were a consequence of pressure from the haemorrhage.

Cesare and Pat dropped everything, took Jack and drove straight to Perth when they heard the news. Urgent draining of the bleed was required to save her life. Jack signed the documents for his wife, and they prepared her for surgery. An external ventricular drain was inserted to relieve the symptoms. However, complications set in and due to the aneurysm's location and quantity of blood leakage, a permanent shunt was necessary. Further surgery was carried out urgently.

Grief-stricken, the family waited at home for phone calls with a report of the findings. Cesare and Pat continued to stay in Perth with Jack and found accommodation nearby for easy access each day. Steve and Sheryl arrived at the hospital early on Saturday afternoon, it had been a long four and a half hour drive to contemplate the prospect of what they'd find when they got there.

The lift doors opened into fluorescent-lit corridors of grey linoleum floors and green painted walls. Clean linen sat on trolleys, and laundry bags full of soiled sheets hung off one side. Other carts had trays of covered dishes to deliver to patient rooms. The signs led them to the right place. They were in the waiting room while the doctor was with Emily. He wanted to speak to the family when he finished his examination of the patient. The neurologist drew a diagram to explain how an aneurysm would have looked before it ruptured. The bleed in the brain had caused swelling which damaged the brain's function. How much damage it had caused was yet to be determined, and it was a matter of time to discover what impact it would have on Emily. Unfortunately, there was a strong likelihood it was quite severe.

"Would it have made any difference if Mum had been sent to Perth sooner?" Pat asked.

"No, she would still be the same. There was nothing else that could be done," the doctor shook his head. Five people sat in the consulting room, speechless. Dark clouds loomed on their horizon. They were in emotional turmoil as they absorbed the prognosis from the specialist. Jack was in denial, she would get better. He just knew she would. She had to, it was unbearable to think otherwise.

Holding hands, Pat and Sheryl entered her private room, tears wet their faces.

"Mum, we have some good news to tell you." Emily looked at them. "Nadia has had her baby, a little boy, Mum. He was born on Thursday, the 2nd of June, and they are both well, you are a Nonna again." There was a spark of recognition in her eyes, both girls saw it. It definitely happened, they were sure of it. Steve walked in with Cesare and was shocked. His Mum had her hair shaved off one side of her head, a large wound was stitched over the bump where the shunt had been inserted, and her pallor was grey. It was not what he expected.

Cesare, Pat and Jack trudged back to the six-bed hostel room. Steve and Sheryl left the building, holding hands, and walked along Murray Street to where their car was parked a block away. Steve's grip tightened, disbelief and sadness emanated from him. His wife cut into his thoughts.

"It's okay to be upset, hon. Your Mum is seriously ill, you can allow yourself to feel the pain." Steve cried, and she wept with him. They drove around to the apartment building and joined the others.

Jack was spent after days of tortured waiting and not understanding what had happened or why. He was exhausted from all the worry and had to lie down after a cup of tea. Before long Jack was sound asleep and snoring.

Pat had been a tower of strength to them; she took the brunt of the responsibility and communication between doctors, nurses and family. Cesare was on annual leave, and they offered to stay in Perth until he had to go back to work. A decision about what they would do beyond that time needed to be made. The brothers and their wives discussed what would be the best course of action to take. It was too expensive to stay in Perth, and the men had to go to work. No-one had any idea how long they would need to do this. Jack would be better off at home in Albany for a break after two days vigil in the hospital. It broke his heart every time he had to witness the sad demise of his precious wife.

Ces and Pat went downstairs to the public phones in the foyer and rang Rosie. Cesare spoke to his sister.

"Hi Rose," his voice caught on the raw emotion in his words. "Mum's not doing too well. We have to...," he broke down. Pat caressed his arm and took the phone from him.

"Hi Rose, sorry, this is very hard. We all have to sort out what we're going to do. We don't know how long Mum will be here, but we expect it will be for some time yet."

"We've talked with Steve and Sheryl, and we think we've worked out a plan." She explained their thoughts. Rosie would talk to the rest of the family about sharing trips to Perth each weekend to take Jack up to visit Emily. She rang back an hour later, everyone agreed to the arrangement. Relieved one decision had been made flooded over Pat, now they just had to get through one day at a time.

"Basta! Basta!" Emily shouted at the nurses. They smiled at each other across the bathtub. At last she had spoken, and that was a good sign.

"We are bastards, aren't we? Sorry love." Emily was returned to her bed in the ward with her hair washed, body bathed and dried and dressed in a fresh nightie. The routine sponge bath had been the only wash she'd had for weeks. Physiotherapists, nurses and doctors traipsed through her day with comments and readings written on her chart. Rosie had gone to Perth during the week and walked into the hospital to find Emily looking much brighter. A nurse came in to check her blood pressure and shunt.

"Hello Rosie, how are you?" she looked at her and smiled. "Emily called us bastards yesterday when we gave her a bath." A twinkle in her eye accompanied her comment.

"What did she say?" Rosie thought it unusual her mother would use such language.

"Busta, Busta," the nurse mimicked Emily.

"No, that's not *'bastard',*" Rosie continued, "Mum was saying *'That's* **enough!***'* in Italian."

"Oh no, poor love. She didn't want us to keep washing her. I'm so sorry, we had no idea it's what she meant."

"She would've been embarrassed more than anything, I expect," Rosie assumed.

"We'll try to be more diplomatic next time, I promise." The nurse left the room.

"So Mum, you didn't like your bath, but you love having a bath. I guess just not with an audience, hey?" Rosie kissed her mother's soft cheek and patted her hand.

The neuro specialist asked for a meeting with Jack and the others on the weekend. Emily's wound had healed, the shunt worked well, and her progress was at a stage where she could respond to intense physio-therapy to stimulate the brain. There were signs of limited attention spans that warranted this treatment. It was up to the family to decide if this was what they wanted because it was time for her to leave Royal Perth Hospital. The obvious choice was a transfer to Shenton Park Rehabilitation Centre even though it meant continued trips to Perth. They'd done this for a month now, to do it for a bit longer would be okay for Emily's sake. The other option was for her to return to the Albany Hospital but the opportunities for therapy there were limited.

CHAPTER TWENTY-FIVE

The Park and The Lodge

A MUCH SOFTER LOOKING TWO storey building was surrounded by a garden and was less ominous than the multi-storey city hospital. An ambulance pulled up at the covered drop-off zone. Paramedics rolled the trolley into the foyer where nursing staff transferred Emily to a wheelchair and took her to a private room. Paperwork was completed, and charts were clipped to the board at the end of the bed.

Emily sat in bed propped up with a pillow to rest after a morning of stretches to her arms, legs, hips and shoulders. The therapy was to help prevent muscle contraction, weights and splints were used to hold the muscles in a lengthened position. She was exhausted and fell asleep. In the afternoon an occupational therapist massaged her hands and arms and spoke to her in clear, loud commands.

"Lift your arm, Emily. Tap your fingers, Emily. Squeeze my hand, Emily." No response, it was written on the chart. A nurse would come and feed her puréed meals with a spoon. She wasn't on a drip for fluids or food anymore.

"Open your mouth, Emily." Her lips would part, and she could swallow the food.

"Drink from the straw, Emily." She would suck on the straw and swallow the liquid.

Some days there was no response, other days she was alert and had good reactions. A programme was outlined for her day-to-day treatment and care. Signs of a gradual improvement began to emerge.

Cesare and Pat, Jack and Sheryl and Steve arrived to see Emily on a Saturday morning. They followed the signs to the ward where brain-injured patients were treated. Many people were in wheelchairs, some had walking frames and others were strapped into chairs so they wouldn't fall forward. The visitors were shuffled into a waiting room by staff. The wait stretched out to over half an hour, they began to get agitated and started to think the worst had happened. Jack was a nervous wreck by the time a nurse came to get them.

"Okay folks, sorry you've been in here for such a long time, but we wanted to be sure Emily was settled before we take you to see her. Please just wait outside the room and look through the observation window. When we're done, we'll let you in."

Puzzled, they followed the nurse to Emily's room. The family stood in awe as they watched her carefully and slowly lift the fork to put food in her mouth. The nurse loaded it up, and she did it again, unaware that five faces glowed with pride and flowed with tears as they watched the scene unfold before them. Deep sighs were let go, and smiles stretched across their faces as they looked at each other in surprise at her success. The therapy was working, and Jack was so excited it took all his effort not to rush into her room. They'd been told to wait, and that's what they did. What a wonderful message to deliver to the rest of the family.

On another visit, Emily whispered some words. They were difficult to understand, but she'd tried to speak and got frustrated no-one knew what she wanted to say. Therapy continued daily for three months until the maximum time permitted in the public hospital system was up, and Emily needed to be transferred to permanent care somewhere. She was incontinent, unable to walk and had to be lifted into and out of bed and rolled over regularly, so she didn't get bedsores. During the day Emily sat in her wheelchair and only responded to intense and consistent treatment.

Another family discussion threw around the options. Jack desperately wanted her to go home, but the best they could do was for her to return to Albany. He didn't want to accept she would need care he couldn't give her. He was tired and at an all-time physical, emotional and mental low. Emily's responses to treatment had been steady but without any further improvement.

The twin engines of the King Air 300 roared to life. The passenger, escorted by a flight nurse, had been tucked safely into position in the Royal Flying Doctor aircraft. It taxied out to the runway and sped into the wind until lift off, undercarriage clunked into the wheel wells, and the plane banked right and headed south. Emily was on her way home. It was a short one hour flight with a smooth touchdown at the airport seven kilometres out of Albany. A waiting ambulance took her to the regional hospital in town.

Her family was excited, Emily was back where she belonged. Of course, it was never going to be like it was before. Tears of joy mixed with the slow grief of knowing this was her life now. They had to wait for an available bed in the permanent care unit, but until then she would be looked after in the hospital. Jack could drive up the road to visit every day. No more torturous trips to Perth.

"Come on, my love, *mange, mange,*" Jack fed Emily her food. It always made people better when they ate properly, that was his theory. He wanted her to get better and come home to him, so they could spend the rest of their lives together like they were supposed to. There were two sipper cups on the trolley table. Jack picked one up and washed it in the sink, dried it with a paper towel and popped it in his coat pocket. He'd need that when she came home, and they didn't have one. Other small items made their way to the top shelf of the pantry cupboard at home as well. Hope was Jack's lifeline, without it he would completely fall apart.

A routine developed where family members shared the load. Emily had a room of her own in the Spencer Lodge facility for patients who were unable to care for themselves. Photographs adorned the walls, and a few favourite trinkets were on the chest of drawers in the hope it would stimulate memories for her. An enlarged copy of the last family photo at Silvana's eldest daughter's wedding took pride of place. Nearly the whole family were in it, two grandchildren were missing, and another was asleep at the time. Nadia was pregnant and didn't know, she thought she had a tummy bug with her queasy stomach that night. Sheryl and Steve's youngest wasn't even a twinkle in the eye yet. Jack and Emily were surrounded by family members crowded in together to fit into the camera lens frame. It was a tight squeeze with 28 happy smiling faces.

Sheryl drove in and parked the car, took the keys out of the ignition and paused with her hands on the steering wheel. It was 11.30am on Tuesday again. Each week it got harder. To coach her thoughts she said inwardly, *'Take a deep breath; this is for Dad and the girls to have a break. Remember, they do it every day - and this is just once a week.'* Emily's Australian daughter-in-law pulled on the handle, got out of the car then closed the door and locked it.

The cement path led to the officious red brick building that loomed ahead of her. The path seemed to get longer each time she came. Her sisters'-in-law were blessed with a natural ability to cope with Emily's care issues, but Sheryl struggled, even though she was willing to help. *'It's because I love you Mum, that it's so difficult. It's not because of you but because of the circumstances,'* she thought again. *'All our hearts grieve to see you sit in the wheelchair unable to speak or do the things you've always done for yourself.'* Her thoughts drifted off into the ether as she psyched herself up to reach for the door handle.

The odour of the elderly and infirm knocked her senses once she entered the foyer. *'It's not their fault; it's just the way it is.'* Dim lighting made it necessary to wait for her eyes to adjust after the bright sunshine outside. She wiped the sweat off her hands with a flower embroidered handkerchief, put a brave smile on her face and went to the dining recreation room.

"Hi Mum, how are you? Oh, you've got your pink cardigan on today. You look pretty. It's time for your lunch." She reached over and kissed Emily on the forehead and gave her a side hug around the shoulders.

Sheryl put the plastic cover over the bowl aside, and had a spoon at the ready.

"I wonder what we have today. Ah, some chicken soup followed by custard for dessert. Yum, that'll be good for you."

"Come on love, open up and have some." A narrow opening of Emily's mouth to take the food was an automatic response when the cutlery touched her lips. A tender stroke on her throat helped remind her to swallow. It was a long process, and any food that dribbled out was wiped away with a face cloth. When Emily had as much food as she would allow past her lips, the pair sat together for a time. Chatter about Steve and her grandsons, and what they were doing at school and work was a one-sided conversation. Every now and then Sheryl had to blink back tears, but emotion still got caught in her voice.

"Bye Mum, I love you. I'll see you later." And it was another farewell until next Tuesday when they'd do this again.

CHAPTER TWENTY-SIX

Mamma

ADRIANA AND NINO'S EYES LOCKED across the table, an indistinct nod acknowledged it was time to tell their family.

"We're going to Australia," Nino announced.

"What? You can't do that." "You're both too old." "No, Nonna, I won't let you go." Responses bubbled out over the top of each other. "What are you thinking, this is crazy."

"Hold on. We're only going for a visit. I want to see my sister, we both need to see Emilia. It's important to your mother too."

"Oh, that's okay." Relief washed over their faces. "We thought you were going to leave Italy and go to live there."

"No, you would've been right. We are too old!"

"Nino is coming." It was a huge journey for Nino and Adriana to take on and not a decision they made lightly. They knew it would be an emotional and difficult visit. It had been over a year since Emily had fallen ill. The family in Australia were abuzz with excitement and plans were put in place for where they would stay and what they would do. Arrangements needed to be sorted for Emily to come out for the day while they were here. Transport, medication, toileting tips and wheelchair access were just some of the aspects they had to consider.

"We're not sure she understands what this is all about, but it'll be a great time to be together again." Jack was pleased with the whole idea and was sure it would rub off on Emily.

The grand day arrived, and family collected Nino and Adriana from Perth Airport for the trek down the highway to bring them to Albany. They were exhausted after twenty-four hours of flying, airport transfers and driving south. Rosie dished up some soup to eat, and then they showered and went straight to bed. A fresh start in the morning would be good for everyone.

Emily remembered waiting ... for her seventeenth birthday to be courted ... for her wedding day, because of the war ... for Jack, he would come ... she knew he would ...

Jack took his brother-in-law and wife to Spencer Lodge to see Emily at ten o'clock, just in time for morning tea, which he did on most days. They'd seen photos the family had sent, but it was distressing to see Emily like this in reality. Love overruled the circumstances, and they shared time with her every day while they could.

The Lions community service club's specifically designed minibus pulled up in the driveway at Rosie's house with its passenger strapped securely into the rigging for wheelchairs. Bill Reside opened the rear door, took down the fittings for the ramps and wheeled Emily out of the vehicle into the warm sunshine. It was a beautiful day. The whole family and a few friends gathered for a welcome meal with the international guests, but the star attraction was Emily and it was good for her to be in this family environment. A snapshot captured the moment. Photos of Emily, Nino, Adriana and Jack were put on the wall in her room as a reminder of the special visit.

Polenta and sausage were cooked and abundant food bulged on the table, everyone pitched in and the multitude was fed until full. Coffee was served later in the afternoon while the sun snaked its way between the Venetian blinds that were partially closed. As was customary, singing erupted, probably because of the grappa in the coffee, after red wine and beer with lunch. Italian songs were belted out in spine-tingling tunes. Someone suggested Nino sing Ave Maria. His rich tenor voice reverberated throughout the dining room, and there wasn't a dry eye in the place. Then he sang *'Mamma'* to Emily. Nino was choked with feeling as he sang the Italian words to his sister.

'I am very happy because I am returning to you. My song is telling you it is the most beautiful day for me', and other lines to say: you will stay with me, you'll not be alone anymore. How much I love you and will hold you in my heart.

Not a sound was heard when Nino finished singing the last line. A hoarse whisper echoed the thoughts of everyone in the room.

"We love you Emily, and we'll always be here for you." Fortunately, the blessing of young children broke the intense atmosphere.

"Can we go out and play now?" Of course, they could, and the rest of the family began to make preparations for Emily to be collected and returned to Spencer Lodge.

Outings for the visitors included sightseeing to The Gap where the sea roared relentlessly between the crevices of grey granite rocks. They walked up the steep steps to the memorial on Mt Clarence that Jack had built, and climbed Castle Rock in the Porongorups amongst tall native karri trees.

Emily remembered waiting ... Jack was coming ... from Somma Lombardo ... or Bardonnechia ... maybe it was Montenegro ... she wasn't sure anymore ...

"Hello Rosie and Pat," the nurse greeted them, but her smile faded quickly. "We need to discuss Emily's health today. You know we thought she was dehydrated, and we gave her an intravenous saline drip which has helped, but there is another problem." Rosie and Pat looked at each other while Jack was oblivious to the conversation where he sat with his wife holding her hand. She was the focus of his life and required his full attention.

"The test results came in today, and they show she is at risk of diabetes. We need to give her treatment to keep her blood sugar levels within the normal range." They all agreed to the medication recommended by her doctor. A tablet crushed into her food was included in her diet after they discovered if it was given to her whole, it sat in her mouth undissolved for a long time. They had to explain all this to Jack, who only wanted his wife to get better and hoped it would make a difference so she could come home.

The mourning coach pulled away from St Joseph's church onto Aberdeen Street and followed the hearse along Middleton Road. Tears of grief flowed down sad faces that looked away from each other. Brothers and sisters in mourning, it was so unexpected. The grey day matched the heaviness in their hearts.

It took a slow fifteen-minute drive to get to Allambie Park Cemetery where the priest waited beside the hole in the ground. Alongside was a pile of white sand covered with a green tarpaulin. The pallbearers took deep breaths as they walked beside the hearse to the grave. This was a task they didn't want to have to do, even though it was a privilege to have been asked. The crowd followed along behind, most wore black.

"Ashes to ashes, dust to dust," the priest spoke the words from the Bible, and Jack's coffin was lowered into the ground. Handfuls of dirt were thrown in on top of the jarrah timber lid. They couldn't believe their Dad had gone, he wasn't supposed to be the first one to go.

Jack had complained of a sore leg and thought he'd pulled a muscle, but didn't think it was worth going to the doctor. However, it was a thrombosis. The blood clot had moved, and he suffered a severe stroke that put him in hospital. Nothing could be done, and the whole family were in shock.

Pat, Nino and Adriana had wheeled Jack across from the hospital to the Lodge for a final visit with Emily. Jack was mentally confused, but that didn't matter, it was evident he wasn't going to get better. Her hand pushed him away because she didn't want to see him like that, well that's what they thought she'd probably meant.

Nino and Adriana's hearts broke when they stood by Jack's bed, he'd had another stroke and was quite agitated. It wasn't supposed to be a time to farewell their brother-in-law, but they had to say goodbye. Then they went to see Emily for the last time. Their flight to Italy was due to leave the next day, and they were off to Perth in an hour.

Three weeks later, after another massive stroke, on March 7, 1989 Jack died. Emily would have to be told, but no-one was ready to do that yet. The house had to be sorted, packed up and a decision about its future was to be made. It was too complicated to rent it out, and they had legal issues to deal with. No-one had power of attorney for Emily. The question, *'so what do we do now?'* posed itself in everyone's mind. They were advised an inventory of all the goods and chattels had to be presented to the Supreme Court of Western Australia before any other processes could continue.

Emily remembered ... Jack was gone ... overseas to Australia ... he would tell her when to come ... and she would go ...

The girls got together to go through everything, and there was plenty of it, Pat diligently recorded all the details and monetary values. A few months before Emily's aneurysm she had taken her daughters and daughters-in-law into her bedroom to choose one of her rings they would inherit one day. The girls took home their treasured possessions and wondered if she'd had some premonition her time was nearly up. She was only 65 and they all expected she would live for a long time to come. Pat was given one of Emily's brooches, but she wanted to know her mother-in-law was happy about it. She went to see her.

"Mum," Pat took the jewellery out of its wrapper. "The girls have given me your brooch, is it all right with you that I keep it?" In a rare moment of lucidity, Emily nodded. "I love you, Mum."

"... love you, too ..." a barely whispered response with a slight hand movement to touch her heart. Pat was overjoyed.

Rosie and Aldo planned a trip to Italy in July. There was one thing that needed to be done before they left. Emily needed to be told Jack had gone, her daughters couldn't do it. They preferred not to say anything at all, but Emily had a right to know. Rosie asked Pat to tell her. They plucked up the courage to deliver the news.

"Mum, we're so sorry to have to tell you, but Dad's passed away."

"...I know..." she whispered back. The girls were surprised at her reaction. How could she know, did someone else tell her? They spoke to the staff, no-one had said anything to her because they didn't think it was their place to do that. One nurse remembered Emily shed tears at the time, the only display of emotion she'd ever seen. They checked the records on her chart, yes, she cried at 6.15pm on that very day. The girls got goosebumps; it was the exact time Jack died. Her soul mate had left her, and she knew deep within he was gone.

Weeks of Emily's refusal to eat was wearing the staff and family down. She ended up with an intravenous drip but she repeatedly pulled the tube out. It was only a couple of weeks before Rosie was due to go away. Every second day they took their Mum to Sil's or Rosie's place to feed her, maybe some good old-fashioned Italian fare could tempt her to eat. She tried some but not much, certainly not enough to give her sufficient nourishment.

The doctor believed Emily had lost the will to live. A drip was tried again, but she continued to pull it away. There wasn't anything to be done but wait and see what she would do. Rosie and Aldo left for Italy. Sil, Pat, Nadia and Giuliana endeavoured to encourage Emily to eat.

Time ticked by, and Emily grew gaunt and sickly. They watched over her constantly and cared for her immediate needs. Pat called in every day after work to see her. The time was close, and her body's organs had begun to shut down. The family came to say their final farewells. Strained emotion, tears and hugs were shared among them. It was barely five months since Jack had gone and now they faced losing their Mum, sister, aunt, nonna and biz nonna as well.

Jack was waiting ... for his Emily ... for his love ... to be together forever ... how long he didn't know ... but he wanted her to come ...

Cesare and Silvana kept vigil over their mother. They had both felt a strong urge to be there on that day, the 10th of August. Brother and sister sat on each side of her bed holding her hands while they wept their silent tears. Her breathing was shallow and slow. Gentle words from Ces and Sil caressed her soul. A sense of Pat's words from last evening hung in the air.

"It's alright Mum, you can go and join Dad whenever you're ready."
And so she did.
'Ciao Mamma.'

The Love Chapter

"Love is patient and is kind. Love doesn't envy. Love doesn't brag, is not proud, doesn't behave itself inappropriately, doesn't seek its own way, is not provoked, takes no account of evil; doesn't rejoice in unrighteousness, but rejoices with the truth; bears all things, believes all things, hopes all things, and endures all things. Love never fails."

1 Corinthians 13: 4-8
The World English Bible
Public Domain

DESERT MOUNTED CORPS MEMORIAL
Commemorates members of the
Australian Light Horse, New Zealand
Mounted Rifles, Imperial Camel Corps
and Australian Flying Corps
who lost their lives in Egypt, Palestine and Syria
1916 - 1918

Jack Nostrini (on right) supervises the block lift
for the circular wall construction

Jack built the internal brick wall and guides concrete to fill the cavity

Adam assists Jack to place block and ensure it is level

Monument base with Jack on the 'out of the ordinary' scaffold

The bronze cast statues unpacked from their shipping crates

Jack leads the guide rope as the crane lifts the horse and rider into place

Jack (on left) lays Hartman's quarried stone pavers
between the monument base and the circular wall

Grand Opening Day by Prime Minister Robert Menzies on October 11, 1964